CW01262358

Black's Picture Sports
SNOOKER

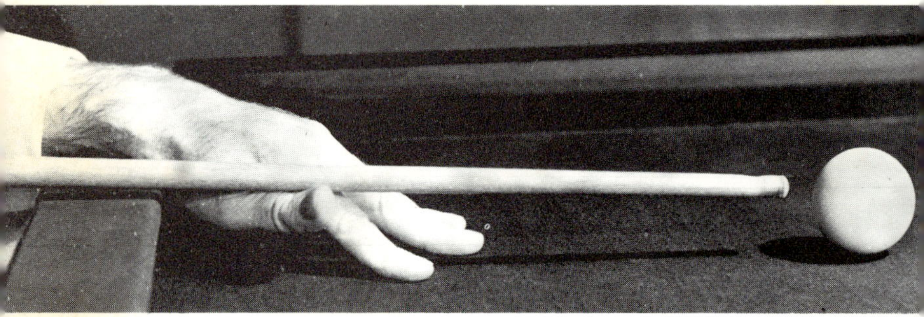

Black's Picture Sports
SNOOKER

Fred Davis

Adam and Charles Black · London

First published 1977 by A & C Black Ltd
35 Bedford Row, London WC1R 4JH

ISBN 0 7136 1740 3

© Fred Davis 1977

Davis, Fred
  Snooker—(Black's picture sports)
  1. Snooker
  I. Title II. Series
  794.7'3   GV900.S6
  ISBN 0-7136-1740-3

Cover Neil Wigley; all photographs Snooker Scene

All rights reserved. No part of this publication may be reproduced, stored in a retrieval system, or transmitted, in any form or by any means, electronic, mechanical, photocopying, recording or otherwise, without the prior permission of A & C Black Ltd.

Set and printed in Great Britain by
Page Bros (Norwich) Ltd, Norwich

Contents

PREFACE 7

1 INTRODUCTION 11
   History of the game 11
   The Game – Snooker 13
   The Game – Billiards 14
   Equipment 15
      Cues 15
      Tips 16
      Rests 16
      Tables 16
   Clothing 16
   Where to Learn 17

2 THE GRIP 19

3 THE BRIDGE 23

4 THE DELIVERY 29

5 AWKWARD BRIDGES 35
   Under the Cushion 35
   Near the Cushion 36
   Along the Cushion 39
   Over a Ball 40
   The Rest 45

6 KEEPING ON LINE 47

7 EYE ON WHICH BALL 49

8	THE SHOTS	51
	Screw	51
	Side	52
	Stun	54
	Swerve	55
9	TOUCH AND FEELING	59
10	POSITIONAL PLAY IS THE KEY	63
11	CHECKING UP ON YOUR STYLE	67
12	YOU CAN ALWAYS IMPROVE	71
13	THE RULES	77
14	USEFUL INFORMATION	89
	Organisations	89
	Book List	90
	GLOSSARY	93

Preface

Like many small boys, I was bought a miniature table one Christmas. Nobody showed me how to play, but I used to amuse myself by knocking the balls round without even having much idea of the rules.

From an early age I was involved in the management of some billiard halls (one of my father's business ventures). By watching and making mental notes and by trying to put into practice what I had seen, I reached quite a good standard on full sized tables and I was entered for the 1925 National Boys (Under 16) Championships when I was 12.

My brother Joe, 12 years my senior, was already one of the top professionals by his twenty-first birthday. He was not only to win the World Professional Billiards Championships four times, but to hold the World Professional Snooker Championship from 1927, when it was first held, until 1946, when he relinquished the title.

Even at that early stage, though, Joe commanded most of the limelight. No one expected me to win my first game but I did and I can remember playing with the great confidence – unjustified as it might have been – with which I have always been blessed. I lost my second game to Sydney Lee, who at 15 was three years older than me, but our first meeting was the start of a friendship which has persisted to this day. Syd went on to win the British Empire Amateur Championship and became a successful touring professional before settling into his present niche as referee for BBC 2's popular snooker series, Pot Black.

Despite my promising debut, I did not play in another

tournament until I was 15 when I won the Boys Championship at my second and last attempt. When I was 16 I became a professional automatically because the stringent amateur regulations of the day meant that anyone, whatever his ability, who had anything to do with the management of a billiard hall could not remain an amateur.

Although I had no obvious immediate incentive, I still played and practised. When I was 18, Joe was asked to enter me for the Junior Professional Billiards Championship. Joe didn't think I was good enough to play, but I won the Championship and retained it the next year, although I played no other matches until I entered the Professional Snooker Championship in 1937.

One problem I had to overcome though was myopia, or shortsightedness. Over a period of a few years, my eyesight gradually deteriorated to the point where snooker balls looked like balls of wool. Rather stupidly, I struggled on until a very moderate professional named Withers beat me in the Professional Championship.

Better late than never, I then consulted an optician who fitted me with a pair of swivel lens spectacles which immediately made me think that snooker, after all, was an easy game. Adjusting to spectacles can be a problem but unless a player's sight is perfect this adjustment has to be made sooner or later. It is difficult to play in ordinary spectacles as the rim tends to hinder your sight of the ball as you stoop down for your shots so, if you can possibly afford it, invest in a pair of swivel lenses which are equipped with a small hinge. This will enable you to tip your spectacles up to an angle which will allow you unimpeded vision.

In 1940, I beat Sidney Smith, who was then ranked number two to Joe, and only lost 37–36 to Joe in the final. Just as I was getting going, the war intervened – but after 1945 I started to progress again and when Joe retired from championship play in 1947, after holding the title continuously for 20 years, most people expected me to win it. In fact, I lost in the final to Walter Donaldson, a Scotsman with a ramrod straight cue action, who produced the most consistent long potting I have ever seen to beat me 82–63.

I had my revenge in the 1948 Championship, in one of the many finals I played at the Blackpool Tower Circus. I went on to win the title nine times in all plus one unofficial world title in Canada, but none of these successes gave me the intense satisfaction I experienced from beating Joe on level terms – three times – for no other player beat him on level terms in his entire career.

My snooker life has not consisted entirely of highlights. I have lost matches. I have spent years, night after night, slogging round the club exhibition circuit playing on all sorts of tables in all sorts of places. I even kept going during the most depressing period in the game's history: from the late 50s when it nearly died to the end of the 60s when it once again regained popularity.

What sustained me – and still does – was my love of the game. It is the most precious asset a player can have. As long as he is fascinated by the game, crying out to play, trying to figure out ways to improve, he is bound to progress provided his basic technique is sound.

What follows is a guide to the fundamentals of the game. Once you have ingrained these good habits thoroughly into your style, you can explore the infinite possibilities of break building and positional play: without that reliable basic technique, though, the most encyclopedic knowledge of break building is virtually useless. One way that the scene has improved out of all recognition since I was young is that there are many more tournaments – both amateur and professional – to enter. My advice to a young player is to enter all the tournaments he can, playing different opponents under various conditions in a match atmosphere. Watch good players, study how they plan a sequence of shots, and – above all – enjoy yourself.

Peter Bardsley (Sheffield), British Boys champion 1973. An excellent bridge in which the cue runs across both the thumb and first finger for maximum support.

1 Introduction

HISTORY OF THE GAME

The Greeks and Romans played many games with balls and sticks but the first recognisable form of billiards was played, rather like croquet, on lawns in the 1340s.

Initially, a mace was used to propel the balls, at first out of doors and later on the indoor table version of the game, which became popular with the French and English nobility in the fifteenth century.

In the eighteenth century there was a gradual change from using maces, with which the idea was to push the ball with a trailing or raking action, to modern cues. Tips however were not used until a French infantry captain, Mingaud, imprisoned for some years in a Paris goal, experimented so successfully with them that on his release in 1807 he was able to astound all and sundry with his cuemanship.

Chalk, which enabled the leather tip to grip the ball more effectively, was introduced in the 1820s.

Cushions, whose only function originally was to stop the balls falling onto the floor, were stuffed with flox or cotton so that the balls would actually rebound, and then were gradually improved to the point where the modern rubber cushion now ensures a consistent angle of rebound.

By 1840, slate had replaced wood as the table surface over which the cloth was laid. The very earliest balls were made of wood but ivory came into favour with those who played seriously and was used for championships until the mid 1920s. The expense of ivory caused synthetic substitutes to be manufactured as early as the 1870s and once it was realised that composition balls were perfectly reliable, they began to be used more frequently and have been used exclusively since the 1930s.

Originally billiards was either a means of relaxation for the gentry or a gambling game for the masses, and the earliest champions were determined largely on the outcome of money matches.

Snooker was a much later invention. It is generally considered to have originated in India in 1875 though it was not until 1916 that an English Amateur Championship was instituted, and another eleven years before the first World Professional Championships was held – and won by my brother Joe.

The Billiards Association, which came into being in 1885 at a meeting of leading figures among the professionals and chief trade houses, nominally governed the game from that date. Under the changed title of the Billiards and Snooker Control Council it still does govern the amateur side, though the professional body, the World Professional Billards and Snooker Association, has been completely independent since 1970.

There is now more activity in the world of billiards and snooker than ever before. The games are played not only by four and a half million players in the British Isles alone but by large numbers in Australia, New Zealand, Canada, India, Sri Lanka, South Africa, Malta, Hong Kong, Fiji, Thailand, Indonesia, Singapore, Guyana, Trinidad, Kenya, Ghana and elsewhere.

In Britain, there is a comprehensive network of local leagues and competitions and the Billiards & Snooker Control Council annually organise national amateur, junior and boys championships. The games receive substantial television coverage and they have at last been recognised even by those mindful of their early gambling background, as demanding the highest standards of skill, concentration and ingenuity.

The games have also become increasingly popular with

women, many of whom now compete against men in local leagues.

THE GAME – SNOOKER

Snooker is a game played with fifteen red balls, six coloured balls, and one white cue-ball. The object of the game is to score points by potting reds and colours and by extracting penalty points from your opponent.

The player must first hit the white (cue) ball against a red, value (1). If he pots it he is entitled to attempt to pot a colour, the values of which are yellow (2), green (3), brown (4), blue (5), pink (6) and black (7). Once potted, the red balls stay down in the pocket, the colours are put back on the table on their appropriate spots. The reds have to be potted in the sequence – red, colour, red, colour etc. When all fifteen reds have been potted, the colours are attempted in order of ascending numerical value.

Penalty points are awarded for failure to strike the required object-ball; if the cue-ball enters a pocket (an in-off); for striking with the cue-tip any ball other than the cue-ball; for touching with body or clothing any balls in play; for pushing the cue-ball instead of striking it cleanly; or for failing to play with at least one foot maintaining contact with the floor.

The minimum penalty is four points and the maximum seven, depending on which balls are involved in the incident.

A sequence of potted balls (for instance, red, black, red, pink) is known as a break. The highest possible break is 147, obtained by potting red, black for all fifteen reds, and then the colours.

A game is known as a frame, and any number of frames can make up a match, depending on the type of match and the time available.

A snooker occurs when a player who is due to hit a red is left with the cue-ball in such a position that other balls prevent him from doing so with a direct stroke. This also, of course, applies when a colour is the ball on.

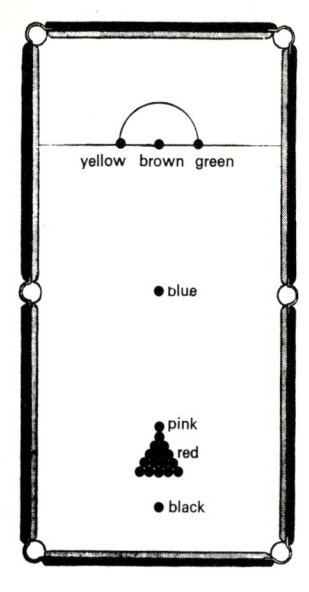

Snooker layout

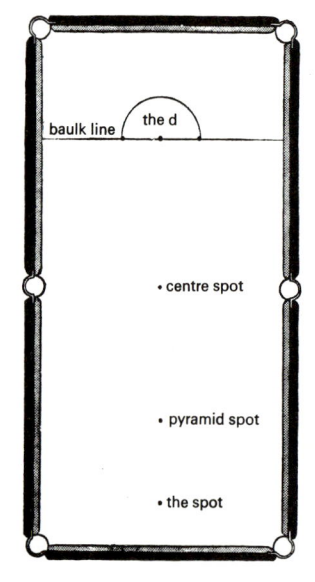

Billiards layout

THE GAME — BILLIARDS

The other most important game which can be played on a billiards table is, of course, billiards. This is a game played with three balls, a red object-ball and two white cue-balls, one of which bears a spot (known as the spot ball) to distinguish it from the other (known as the plain ball). A game consists of either any agreed number of points from 100 up, or a specified length of time, i.e. one hour, two hours – even two weeks!

Points are scored by means of pots, in-offs and cannons (a shot in which the cue-ball contacts the other two balls).

Player A plays all his shots with the spot cue-ball and player B with the plain cue-ball. The non striker's cue-ball thus becomes an object-ball for the striker.

Scoring consists of three points for potting the red, three for an in-off red, two for potting the white, two for an in-off white and two for a cannon.

When the red is potted it is replaced on the billiards spot (the spot which the black occupies in snooker) but the object-white, when potted, remains in the pocket until it is the next player's turn to play.

After scoring an in-off the player may play from any point in the semi-circle known as the D provided the cue-ball travels out of baulk – the baulk line is drawn from one side cushion to the other in the bottom part of the table (see illustration) – before striking the first object-ball.

If the striker fails to contact either object-ball, his opponent is credited with one point. If the cue-ball enters a pocket without striking another ball the non-striker is credited with three points.

Again, any sequence of scoring strokes is known as a break.

EQUIPMENT

Cues The best cues tend to be made of ash or maple. My own cue is over 70 years old and, if you are lucky, you may be able to acquire one of the many wonderful cues made by the craftsmen who were in business around the turn of the century. Of the modern cues, I would particularly recommend the Powerglide range.

Cues should reach just below shoulder height. 4 ft 7 in to 4 ft 9 in is often spoken of as the best length, but a few inches either way are less important than personal preference and the physical make-up of the player, though most professionals tend to play with cues which are shorter than those used by run of the mill amateurs.

It is not always a good idea for a child to attempt to play with a full size cue, as he will find this unwieldy. Far better that the cue should grow as he grows.

Beware of cues which are too whippy, as these have been proved to be unreliable, but in general the choice of cue remains a personal matter. If you feel comfortable with it then it's for you.

Tips Most leading players use Elk Master tips or possibly Blue Diamond. Your tips should be neither spongy nor iron hard but should give your stroke a nice feel as you strike the cue-ball. Your tip should be domed rather than flat and should be regularly chalked – most leading players use Triangle or National Tournament chalk – to minimise the possibility of a miscue.

Rests These are implements which are used to help you play shots which cannot be reached using the ordinary stance. A rest consists of a short stave with an X-shaped head, usually made of steel, through which the cue runs as you aim at the cue-ball. The basic rest is slightly longer than the usual length cue – about five feet. There are also two special rests, which are longer and with which you use a longer than average cue: the half butt is seven feet long and the three-quarter butt nine feet.

Tables All official matches and tournaments are of course played on full size 12 ft × 6 ft 1½ in tables, but there is a great deal of fun to be had from playing on the many tables of smaller dimensions which are available. These are an excellent introduction to the game for a young player, as they will not give him the feeling of being overwhelmed by the area of a full sized table. I began on a miniature table myself, and many other professionals did too – but try to switch to a full sized one as soon as you can.

CLOTHING

Snooker demands no special clothing, though I believe that in matches it is always an advantage to be correctly and comfortably dressed as this is good for your morale if nothing else. Avoid shoes with slippery soles, as you often have to balance delicately on one leg.

WHERE TO LEARN

Many players learn to play on miniature tables in their own homes. Others do so in youth clubs and a few have access to tables in general purpose clubs. Many specialised snooker clubs go out of their way to cater for young players. The Lucania chain in the South of England, for instance, organises its own Junior championships.

The Billiards and Snooker Control Council runs a coaching scheme from its headquarters in Huddersfield (see page 91). The B&SCC will also provide entry forms for the Boys (Under 16), Junior (Under 19) and English Amateur Championships.

Photo 1. The Grip

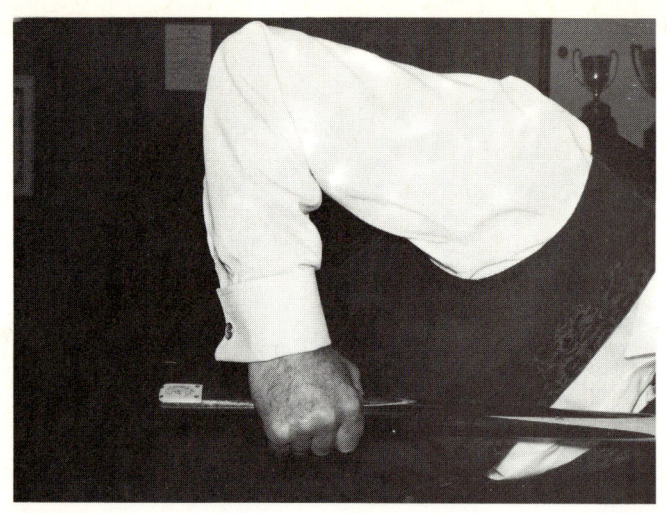

The cue should be held — not too tightly and not too loosely — a few inches from the end of the butt, though for shots which you can only just reach without the aid of the rest, it may be held at the end.
The wrist to elbow should be perpendicular though in practice, a small deviation from this classic ideal does not seem to matter. For instance, I have my arm slightly forward of vertical as I address the cue-ball for a shot.
The danger of starting with your cue-arm slightly forward of vertical is that you can take more backswing but can obtain less follow through.
The contrary danger — which is much more serious — is that if you start with the cue-arm behind the vertical you can obtain as much follow through as you like but very little backswing — which limits your cue power.

2 The Grip

I hold my cue in a solid grip: probably I have the firmest grip of all the leading professionals. What I do may not be right for you to copy, for snooker is played well in many styles and by many theories. One still occasionally sees people playing snooker with the old fashioned piccolo grip which was once fashionable in billiards, especially with players who specialised in a delicate type of play. With this grip the cue is held by the tips of the fingers, but this is quite unsuitable for the punch and power shots which are so important in snooker.

At the same time, a fierce clutch is bad. It is bad to do anything that sets up tension. What is needed is a firm grip with all four fingers wrapped round the butt (Photos 1 and 2). In my case, I have a tendency to turn the cue hand inward very slightly so that the cue is probably not directly beneath the elbow, as it should be. This tendency comes, perhaps, through having a firm hold on the cue. It doesn't affect my accuracy but it isn't necessarily the sort of thing to copy. I do see many other players with their hand turned inward, some a great deal more than my own. I also see players who have the reverse tendency: namely to turn the knuckles of the cue hand outward, and this I am quite sure is wrong because it means a loss of power and control.

The main reason for a firm grip is that it helps promote the correct action whereby, for all ordinary strokes, the wrist should not flex. The stroke is made with the forearm, wrist, hand and cue all in one piece. Only at the end of the stroke is the wrist affected. Players who use the piccolo

Photo 2. The Grip

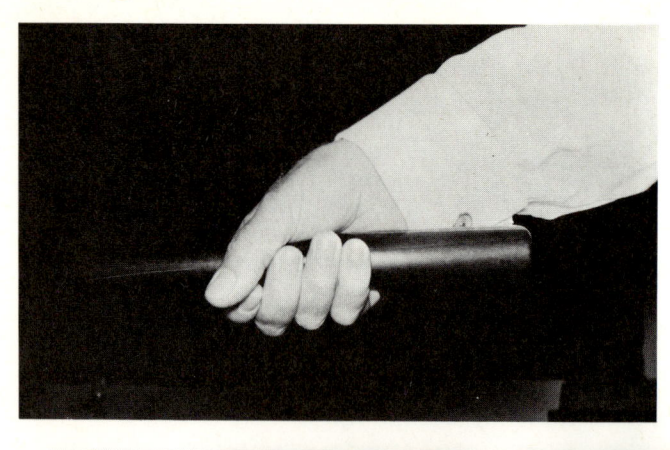

A

B

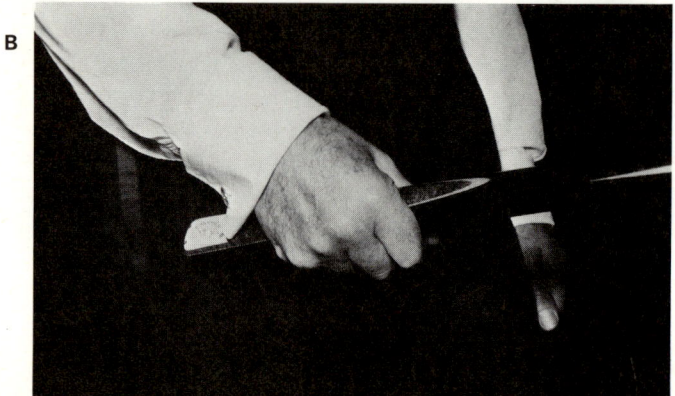

A and B show that the grip with which I pick up my cue is the same that I actually use for my shots.

Note that I am grasping the cue with all four fingers as if about to hit someone over the head with it.

The cue is held with just enough strength to lift it from the table. Anything tighter tends to interfere with the fluency of your cueing; anything looser tends to make the action uncontrolled and floppy.

grip usually have a floppy wrist as well, so that instead of the whole forearm swinging the hand tends to swing from the wrist.

At the end of the normal stroke the hand should turn downwards and, indeed, if it doesn't do so, the cue must finish up in the lampshade. To finish with the cue practically on the cloth the hand must turn so that it looks, and feels, as though you have been striking with the base knuckle of the forefinger. I find that during the preliminary swings the grip is, or seems to be, equally distributed among the four fingers, but that at the moment of striking I am actually hitting with the forefinger and thumb. This seems to give maximum power with minimum effort, which is what one wants, and also to make the action rather like a boxer's short punch instead of a long swing. That too, is the ideal action for snooker.

Many years ago, in an old textbook, I read in the first chapter – 'Put your cue on the table, then pick it up one-handed, by the butt. The way you then hold the cue is the way you should hold it when you play.' This advice remains true in regard to the strength of the grip.

Bill Blake (Newport, Isle of Wight). A tall player who nevertheless gets as low as possible on his shot. Note the widely spread fingers of the bridge hand, the lower left arm resting on the table bed, the cue making a slight indentation in the chin and the eyes looking intently along the line of the shot.

3 The Bridge

In most games the newcomer gets some instruction at the start. Boys are taught football and cricket at school, and most people taking up golf either take lessons from the pro before they play a round, or experiment on the course, lose a dozen expensive golf balls, and then rush to the pro for help.

But most people will take a cue from a rack and try to play billiards or snooker without any clue as to the proper technique. They look very odd, usually clutching the cue at the very end of the butt, holding it high and digging down as they strike. Gradually, by trial and error and by watching others, they fall into better ways; but they can also fall into some bad playing habits which may stay with them for life.

The unfortunate thing is that a player cannot see himself as we see him. If he could, what a lesson he would learn.

But some things he can see. For instance, he can see the bridge he is making. In the course of a year I visit perhaps a hundred or more clubs, and see and play against players of all grades. The number of hopelessly bad bridges I see astonishes me. Even the club champion, sometimes, will screw up his bridge hand into a shapeless lump and poise the cue perilously in a shallow little channel between the thumb knuckle and the base of the first finger.

I admit this proves it's possible to play well with a bad bridge, but I also know very well that any player would do better with a good bridge. This particularly applies to the average or below-average player. The first thing a

Photo 3. The Bridge

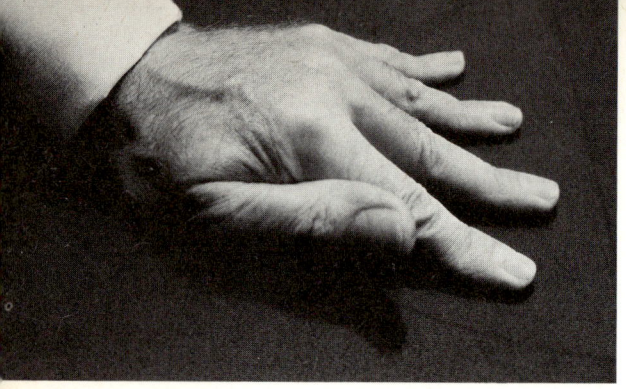

The bridge is formed by creating a firm channel between the thumb and first finger.
Place the left hand on the table, fingers widely but not uncomfortably spread and cock the thumb.
Grip the cloth with the pads of the fingers so that the hand is immovable on the shot itself.
As the thumb is cocked, the knuckles of the fingers become slightly raised.
The hand continues to rest solidly on the heel and the fleshy underpart of the thumb.

good bridge does for you is to hold your stance firmly. Not many players realise that in fact the bridge hand is the front leg of the tripod which keeps the whole body steady, the other two being your two legs.

Any player who has double-jointed fingers has a big advantage because he can make a particularly strong bridge. So can men with long fingers. That outstanding Australian player of the 40s and 50s, Horace Lindrum, credited by some with the most powerful bridge in the world, had double-jointed fingers and although he was a man of no great physique, no one could force a shot harder. His fingers bent downwards as he made his bridge, and you could see the blood leaving his knuckles under the pressure.

The way to make a good bridge is simple enough (Photo 3). Lay your hand flat on the cloth, spread your fingers as wide as possible and stretch them taut. Then draw the finger pads inwards, causing the hand to hump. Cock the

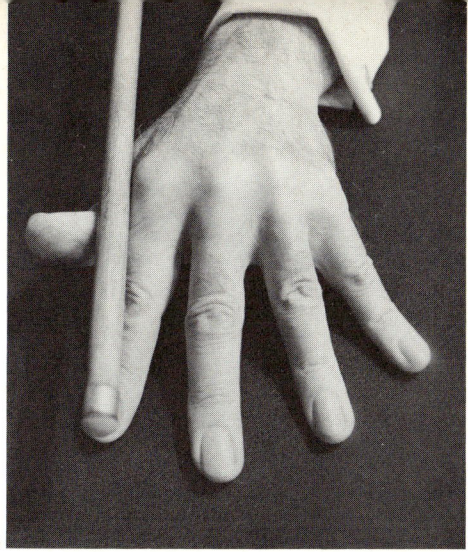

Photo 4. The Bridge
The cue is then placed in the channel between thumb and forefinger in such a way that additional support is given to the cue by the first finger. In preparing for a shot, a number of preliminary addresses are made during which the action of the cue is grooved to go forwards and backwards in a perfectly straight line before making the shot itself.

thumb high, thus forming a comfortable channel through which the cue will ride (Photo 4). Two other points remain. One is that the finger pads must really grip the cloth, so that the hand is quite immovable – it is this gripping which causes the knuckles to whiten. The other is that the bridge arm must be thrust out straight, giving you the feeling of a broom handle with a broom on the end, the broom being the bridge hand. Now you have the feeling of tautness. Keeping the fingers well splayed and pressing hard, and the thumb properly cocked, you will find it much easier to line up for the shot, and much simpler to keep still on the shot.

This should be your bridge for all ordinary strokes. But there are many occasions when the conventional bridge cannot be used. I notice for example a tendency to avoid making a bridge against the cushion when the cue-ball is a foot or so out. Players insist on getting the bridge hand on the cloth, even though it is obviously too

**Photo 5.
The Bridge**

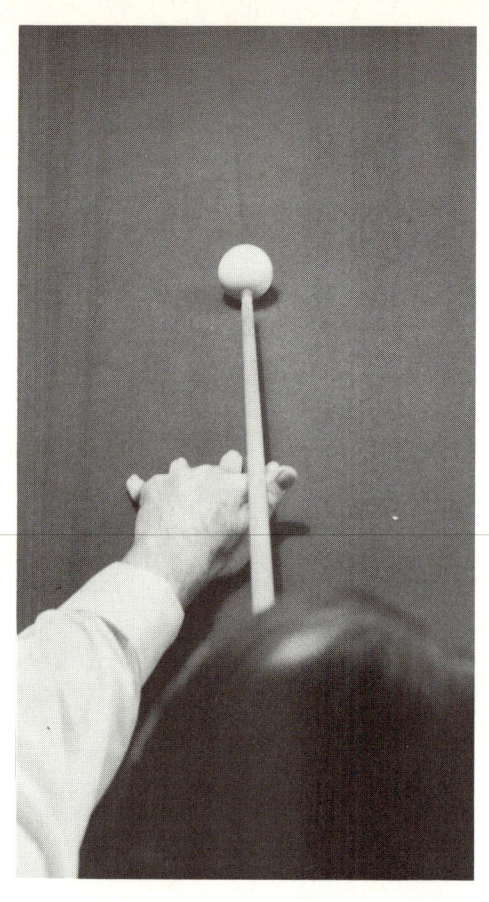

A

close to the ball, rather than face making the straightforward cushion bridge (see also Chapter 5).

This latter is made by placing your four fingers on the wooden ledge and then dropping your wrist below it. When you have done this, you will find that by cocking your thumb you will have made your channel quite comfortably, and although the cue is running over the cloth of the cushion you do not have that 'lost and wandering' feeling. You should try this bridge and, even if you miss a shot or two, persevere, as all will soon be well if not better.

B

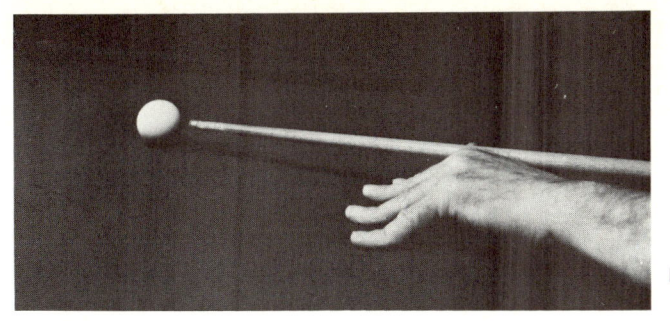

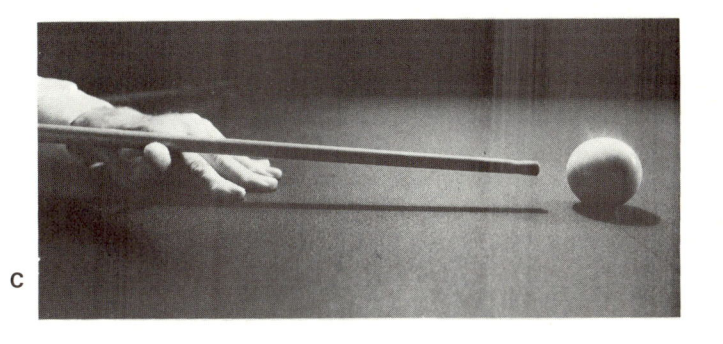

C

A, B and C show the bridge from behind and from the side. They reiterate the points previously mentioned and also establish the distance of the bridge hand from the cue-ball — some seven to eight inches.

Bridging over intervening balls is rarely done well by anyone below championship level. Lesser players get nervous and poke at the ball over a hurried makeshift bridge. A good player makes few mistakes if he can get two finger pads on the cloth, for this is enough to let him establish a grip for general stability. The rest of the shot lies in cocking the thumb well and refusing to be too ambitious.

Photo 6. The Bridge

A

B

Like most professionals, I stretch out my left arm straight as I take my stance for a shot.
Some players, notably John Spencer, twice world champion, play with their left arm slightly bent but this can make it more difficult to keep the bridge hand flat on the table.
A straight left arm tends, more easily than a bent one, to rest on the table to give the bridge additional steadiness and support.

4 The Delivery

Some people appear to have a good, straight steady cue action from the first moment they start to play. Within a few games they are banging down all the so-called easy ones without any trouble, and they get ahead with the rest of the game much quicker than others because they do not have to worry overmuch about whether the ball is going down or not. Others have potting troubles all their lives – even men who are good at the other departments of the game; players whose strength is good, who have an uncanny knowledge of the angles and who can lay a deadly snooker. It is almost pitiful to see them make a lovely positional shot and then fail to knock the colour in.

One of the reasons for their difficulty is a badly made bridge; another is a habit of moving some part of the body on the stroke. But there are players who conform in these respects and still cannot rely on their potting. They tell you that one day it seems easy but that the next even the simple shots are difficult. These players suffer from cue wobble. I should think the percentage of people with this problem is very high indeed, and the odd thing (well, it seems odd to me) is that players who have been at the game for twenty years and play reasonably well at a club standard still suffer from it.

This is a complaint which you may never have or you may always have – unless you know how it is caused. It depends at the outset of your playing career on how you pick up, and hold, your cue. This, in turn, depends on the length of your cue and its balance. Much of the trouble of side to side wobble is caused by having the cue-hold too far back. Ideally, the book tells us, the forearm, at rest, should drop perpendicularly from the elbow and the grip should be one inch from the end of the butt. But it is ridiculous to lay down such rules. Cues in any club rack vary in length up to nine inches, and in weight as much as three ounces. Players' arm lengths vary.

I believe in a short, sturdy cue; not because I am short, but because I believe a short cue is better for snooker than a long one. Short back action means greater accuracy in the drive. I also believe in the cue-hold being slightly in front of the vertical, but I see many, many players whose grip is behind the vertical. When I point this out, they are surprised: they didn't know. I like to get as close to the shot as possible, because I find that the closer I get the more control I have over what I am doing. The long sawing movements with long cues, with flowing finishes, are not for this game. Snooker requires compactness.

I believe in a short backswing and a good follow through but even the follow through must be strictly controlled and the cue held rigidly on line. A good follow through doesn't mean a flowing, meandering action. I like to be well forward over the left knee to get into the shot, but this may not suit you – it depends on your height.

Another important point is to keep the cue running close to the body – that is, brushing against the waistcoat without being buried in it. All these factors make for compactness – elbow well up, hand slightly in advance of elbow, good solid grip on the cue, hand wrapped well round the cue, and no pencil grip: these build up to a short, level, reasonably wobble-proof cue movement (Photo 7). If you have any wobble at all you must get rid of it, and at once you will know the joys of really good potting.

One further point: many players have cue wobble because they stand facing the shot too squarely. Stand at an angle of 45 degrees. The turning of the trunk to face the line of the shot causes some necessary tightness and tension, which all helps to fix the stance firmly.

I often think, especially after I have played a shot I

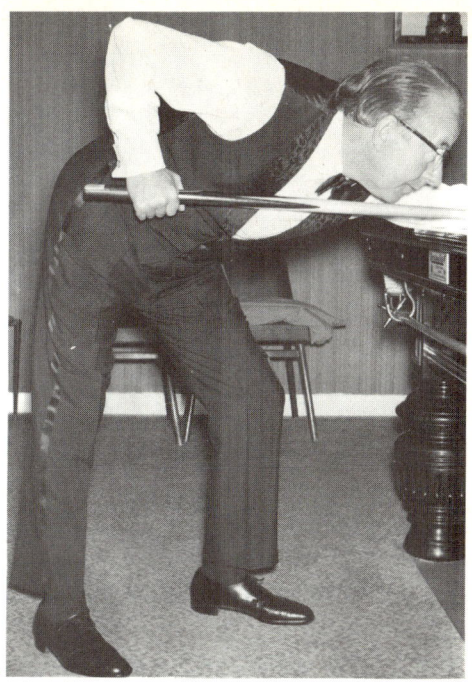

Photo 7. The Stance
The position of the feet is vital in keeping the body absolutely still as the shot is made.
The front (left leg) should be bent and taking most of the player's weight. The left foot should be pointing in the direction of the shot.
The right leg should be braced and straight with the right foot taken round just far enough to give stability to the stance, without being taken round so far that the player becomes 'chest on' to the shot.
The cue should run as near horizontally as possible and should lightly brush the chin in order to bring the eyes as close as possible to the line of the shot.
The cue should also brush the chest lightly as an additional aid to keeping the cue on line.

know to have been a bad one, of the little three part warning which the starter gives to children lined up for a race: 'One to be ready, two to be steady, three to be off'. The second line perhaps is not important to the runner, but to the snooker player it is so vital that one ought to keep it in one's mind all through the match. As in golf, and in fact all games where the striker has to contend with a 'dead' ball instead of a moving one, the accuracy of the stroke depends, more than anything else, on the steadiness and position of the head when contact is made.

I think I owe much of my success to the fact that I do keep still on the shot. Moreover, I do so without conscious strain. I feel that if you screw yourself into some taut position, like a golfer with an eccentric putting stance, in order to clamp yourself rigidly, this is unnatural and will affect your game in the long run. Rhythm and timing are affected and these are the essentials of good snooker.

Most snooker players know the recognised stance, with the weight forward over a bent knee and the body facing half right. But don't let us be dogmatic about this. Plenty of very useful players have unorthodox stances.

There is an appreciable difference, for instance, between my stance and that of the great Scottish player Walter Donaldson. I should know for I had many hard battles with him. I am broad. He was slim. I turn my body to the right and face more to the shot. His action was smooth, unhurried and long in the finish, with a leisurely pause before he looked around to see what had happened. There was not a trace of movement anywhere except in the cueing arm and shoulder. Yet a smoother striker of the ball you will never see.

I have seen professionals who are apt to move, but Alex Higgins is the only one who does who has got into the top flight. In clubs I see players in all manner of strange stances. A favourite one is to sit back on the haunches with feet square and wide spread, sometimes with both knees bent. Another is to have one foot lined up behind the other. Some players have their feet very close together and others find comfort in turning the toes of both feet inwards. The essential thing is to be comfortable in a position which you can maintain with absolute steadiness when the cueing arm goes forward. If you can't, you must find another stance.

Strictly according to theory, nothing except the forearm and upper arm should move, not even the eyes, until the cue has come to rest. In practice, this isn't possible because the forward thrust of the cue starts the whole of the upper part of the body moving upwards, but it's a good thing to keep the theory in mind and to get as near as possible to the ideal of a perfectly stationary head, trunk and legs.

What can help a great many players is the little recitation of the starter. The temptation is often – particularly when the stroke is difficult – to take a long time over the preliminaries and then suddenly to dash the shot off, as though trying to catch the moment of accuracy in midair. Most players do this when there is some awkward cueing to be performed or when there is a great danger of the cue-ball following the object-ball into the same pocket from a long range shot. The natural urge is to poise the cue and get rid of the shot as quickly as possible, hoping it will turn out all right. Of course, it seldom does.

It's the old story that the man who controls himself can conquer anything. If you can control the cue sufficiently to dictate when and at what speed the stroke will be made, your chance of accuracy rises enormously. This is hard to do. One thing you must remember is to slow down your preliminary waggles to the speed at which you finally intend to push the cue through. The other is that you must consciously pause but without stopping the cue. Try saying to yourself: 'One to be ready, two to be steady . . . and smoothly through the ball'. If you do that, I am willing to wager you will be pleasantly surprised to find how still you have managed to keep. It may seem a small thing but to the average player it can be worth as much as two blacks per frame.

Photo 8. Awkward Bridges – Under the Cushion

A

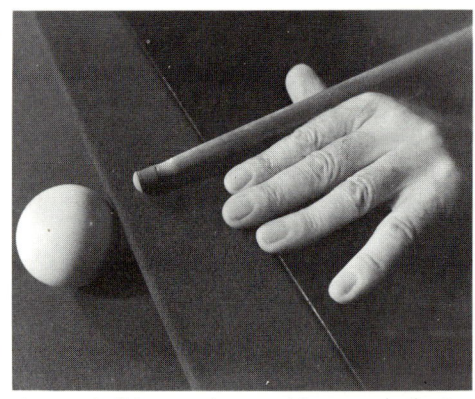

B

No player likes playing the cue-ball from under a cushion as only the top part of the ball can be struck.

To play from this position the cue is elevated slightly above the horizontal position to reduce the risk of a miscue.

If the cue travelled on a horizontal line it would merely brush over the top of the ball, but with the elevation shown it is possible to strike the cue-ball cleanly as the cue, on its downward motion, misses the cushion cloth by a fraction on impact with the ball.

It is most important to keep the bridge firm and this is best done by pushing the bridge hand hard onto the cushion rail, so that the left arm is taking most of your body weight.

5 Awkward Bridges

Snooker is a game of recurring positions, but some positions naturally recur more frequently than others. Gradually you come to know the awkward ones which you nearly always miss, and prominent among these is the pot which requires the striker to play directly away from a cushion, with the cue-ball tucked close.

This sometimes occurs on the black, when the cue-ball is against a side cushion and more or less straight behind the black in line with a top pocket. More frequently it crops up for centre pocket pots. You pot your red into a top pocket intending to bring the cue-ball nicely behind the blue, but it runs wide, just misses the centre pocket and comes to rest just above or below it. The blue is on its spot, the pocket opposite yawns at you, and you feel you are expected to have no trouble at all. In your own heart, you know perfectly well you are very likely to miss it. Furthermore, you know you will miss by over-cutting.

This shot, it may comfort you to know, is detested just as much by the professional as by you. It is difficult because there is only a small patch of the cue-ball to hit, and that is the top surface. Therefore, you cannot strike horizontally, and you cannot play comfortably into the centre of the ball, where most snooker shots are played. You find you must raise your cue-butt and strike downwards, otherwise you will miscue. Carefully though you play, the apparently simple task of moving the cue-ball straight for three feet is amazingly elusive.

Perhaps it will help if you understand what is happening. It amounts to this: when you strike downwards on the top of the ball, you make the ball bounce. Not perceptibly, but nevertheless it does leave the table. It is a miniature

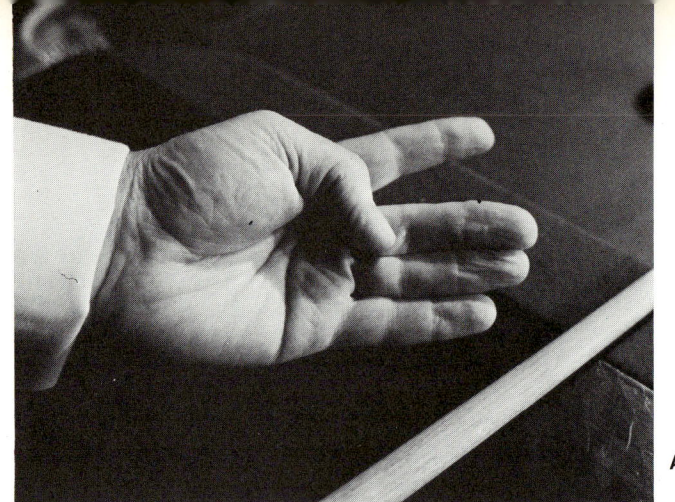

A

B

C

example of the power steeplechase shot (now barred except for trick shots) in which, by striking a really hard downward blow, driving the ball into the bed of the table, you can cause the cue-ball to jump a ball a yard or four feet away. In the comparatively slow stroke we are discussing, the ball may leave the cloth by no more than a sixteenth of an inch. The important thing is, it does hop, and this causes deviation.

Faults arise in playing away from under a cushion from firstly, raising the cue-butt too high, and secondly, failing to realise that follow through is now absolutely vital. If your cue is well tipped, and if you play into the ball instead of trying to skim it, there is no need to raise the hand very much. As direction is simple and the pocket wide, you can afford to concentrate on correct impact of tip on ball, and this you must do. The higher you raise the butt, the worse the direction is likely to be. You will avoid miscueing if you remember to play well through and of course to strike centrally. The slightest deviation from centre is fatal.

It is important to observe what happens at all times. For example, if you always overcut, and you still do this even after you have played according to my instructions (Photos 8–12), then obviously you are still making a mistake somewhere. My advice is – make the necessary allowance for error. In other words, aim to pot the ball on the top side of the pocket. Allow for your error.

This may sound sheer heresy. But snooker is a game of illusions and deceptions. I will confess here and now that for certain pots I always make an allowance for my own error, even though I don't know why it should be necessary. I know, for instance, that I have a tendency to over-

Photo 9. Awkward Bridges – Near the Cushion
When the cue-ball is near the cushion – too near to allow the bridge hand to be placed on the table in the normal way – a loop bridge is formed by tucking the thumb underneath and running the cue between this and a raised first finger.
The cue should be lightly brushing both the back of the thumb and the back of the finger to keep it on line.

Photo 10. Awkward Bridges – Near the Cushion
When the cue-ball is slightly further from the side cushion but still not far enough to allow enough space for the bridge on the table bed, the bridge hand is advanced so that the fingers are actually clutching the inside of the cushion rail.
Note that the left arm is bent for this shot.

Photo 11. Awkward Bridges – Near the Cushion
When the cue-ball is yet another inch or so from the cushion but still not far enough to allow space for the normal bridge, the cushion rail can come in handy to support the wrist as shown here.
The fingers are gripping the cloth firmly and these, together with the comfortably placed wrist, will ensure a firm bridge even though the palm of the hand is not actually resting on the bed of the table.

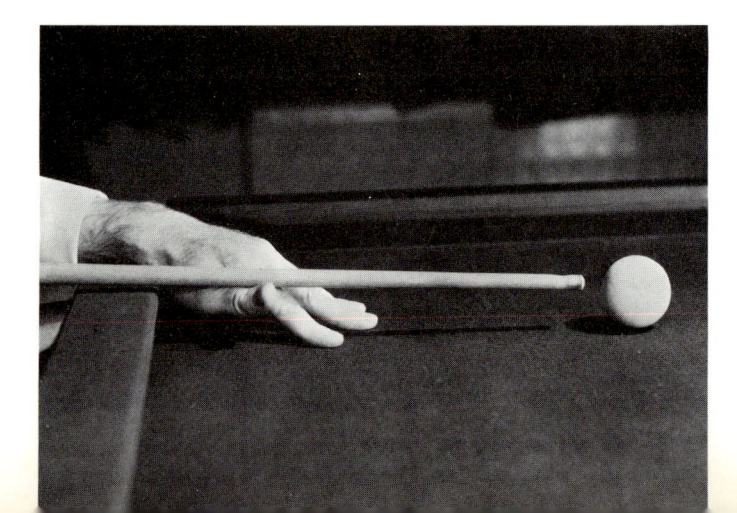

Photo 12. Awkward Bridges – Along the Cushion
Shots in which the cue has to run obliquely across the cushion rail can be awkward but should be approached with a variant of the loop finger bridge – in this particular position by folding the finger under the cushion rail.

cut if cutting a ball to a right hand pocket, but not if towards a left hand pocket. Maybe there is some drift that way, or possibly it happens to all right handed players.

Whatever the reason, I have failed to discover it, so I allow for it. I think if you still miss this awkward one from under the cushion, and invariably by over-cutting, then you should allow for it in lining up your aim. In any event, you stand to lose nothing.

Quite a different position and apparently an even easier one, which often goes wrong to an amazing degree for the ordinary player is that in which the right handed player has to stand on the right side of the table and lean over to play towards the top end. From the left hand side he is comfortable and confident; from the right hand side, leaning the wrong way, as it were, he misses his pot by a margin which quite staggers him. 'Such an easy one!' he says ruefully. The reason is that, leaning partly backwards, and perhaps not leaning sufficiently, the player does not have the elbow, wrist, chin and cue-hand all in line. Something is hanging out to dry! The answer is: use the rest.

A

B

C

Photo 13. Awkward Bridges – Over a Ball

When another ball intervenes between cue-ball and bridge hand, the bridge and cue naturally have to be elevated in order to make a clear stroke at the cue-ball.

The angle of elevation needed will depend on how close cue-ball and intervening ball are.

If they are very close (as in A) the last four fingers of the bridge hand should be almost as perpendicular as you can make them.

The first finger is drawn up slightly to help support the thumb as it forms a channel for the cue.

Because the cue is elevated you need to stand almost upright though, of course, head and shoulders are bent as the eyes look along the line of the shot.

The cue-tip should just miss the intervening ball as it strikes the cue-ball. The nearer the cue-ball is to the intervening ball the closer the bridge hand should be to the intervening ball.

In B the cue-ball is several inches from the intervening ball and therefore neither the bridge nor the cue needs to be elevated to the same degree.

Indeed, it is even possible to give the bridge arm extra stability by resting the elbow on the bed of the table.

As in A, however, the weight is well forward and the fingers of the bridge hand are really digging into the cloth.

In C there is almost but not quite room to place the bridge hand between the intervening ball and the cue-ball.

Therefore, I employ a slightly raised version of the normal bridge with the angle of elevation still less than in B but the left elbow again giving the bridge arm additional support.

**Photo 14.
Stretching**

A

In stretching sideways for a shot it is important to get not only the eyes but as much as possible of the shoulder and arm behind the shot.

This is why, in A, I have hoisted my right leg on to the table so that my hand and shoulder are in the same position as they would have been, had I been able to stand for this shot in the normal way.

In B, where the cue-ball has been taken a couple of ball widths to the right, I am on the verge of overstretching.

My arm is not behind the cue in the normal way (as it is in A) but I still have enough control over my cue-hand to push the cue through straight. Unusually, I use the bouclée bridge (see also Photo 19, page **52**) in this position as an aid to stability.

On the whole, however, B shows not so much a method to copy but an instance where a player has developed his own style through precise control of his arm in an awkward position.

In this position, indeed, it may well be preferable to use the rest, as I myself am forced to in C when the cue-ball is taken yet another couple of ball widths to the right.

B

C

The use of the rest calls for a completely different stance, in which the player stands either chest on (as I do) or even with the right shoulder leading in a sideways position (almost akin to that for a tennis backhand) which other players prefer.

The rest is secured by keeping the left hand firmly on top of it. The eyes, of course, are behind the line of the shot and the cue is pushed through straight, albeit with a sideways motion which is harder to master than the straightforward orthodox swing.

43

Photo 15.

One position in which I prefer not to play with my chin right down on the cue is when the cue-ball and object-ball are very close together.
The slightly elevated view I take here makes the angle of the shot easier to sight.

I also refrain in this kind of position from getting right down on the shot as the slightly elevated view of the balls, I find, makes it easier to assess the relationship between cue-ball, object-ball and pocket.

Photo 16.

**Photo 17.
The Rest**

The grip of the cue in using the rest differs radically from the orthodox grip.
I use two fingers on top and the thumb underneath to generate the power required for the shot with the remaining two fingers underneath merely lending additional support.

The position of my feet using the rest shows the left leg bent and the right leg straight, a stance which I have been able to adopt effectively, though many players find it easier to remain still on the shot (only the lower arm moving) by leaning into the shot with the right leg foremost and the left leg back.

**Photo 18.
The Rest**

Natalie Stelmach (Canada), Canadian's Women's champion 1976. A basically sound action with the rest. She is using a two-piece cue (note the joint in the middle) which is particularly popular with Canadian players, and which is becoming more popular in other parts of the world.

6 Keeping on Line

One danger in trying to help players to improve their snooker is to give them more to remember than is humanly possible. What would I say if I had to restrict my advice to one point only in an expensive cable?

'Keep your head down.' 'Keep still on the stroke.' Good points both, but I would settle for 'Keep cue dead on line at finish of stroke'.

While much advice is given about what should happen before the ball is struck, very little is ever said about what should happen afterwards. But only the exceptional genius has ever managed to get to the top despite a bad finish to his stroke.

The perfect finish is simple enough to describe. The cue, travelling parallel to the cloth, should strike through the ball for several inches and then stop dead, right in the same groove, and either still parallel to the cloth or with the cue-tip resting on the cloth. If that is done, then the object-ball must go down every time if the sighting is correct. Except for long range pots, or pots into closed pockets, where exact sighting is extremely difficult, the sighting of the average player is usually correct. He picks the right angle, but doesn't hit the object-ball at that angle.

When you think that one out, you realise there are other forces at work, for you can hit a chalk mark on the cushion from ten feet ten times out of ten. Yet with a latitude of as much as an eighth of an inch in striking area, to pot a ball from six feet the average player will miss it more often than not. If you can hit the chalk mark, why not the invisible mark on the object-ball?

The chief reason is that your cue-swing is so insecure that as soon as you concentrate on potting, something goes wrong. This you can test by trying your skill at potting a dead straight ball off the centre spot with the cue-ball one foot from the ball, into the top pocket and following through with your cue-ball. This should be easy. Try it again three feet from the ball on the centre spot. Now the result will depend on how good a player you are.

There is another reason: there is a natural temptation, when potting a ball at an angle, to snatch the cue away after contact, in the direction opposite the pocket, as if making sure you are cutting the ball wide enough. Seven or eight times out of ten misses are therefore overcut. Count them yourself when you next play.

How, then, do you gain sufficient control over your cue? It's all in the action. I could take fifty players in any club, one after the other, and improve their play immediately by converting them to an action similar to mine or that of practically any top class player. Put very briefly, it is this: the action must be horizontal; very short but very easy, slow and rhythmic; once started, it must never stop until the actual strike; hand and cue must travel close to the body without hugging it; and finally, on impact, the cue-hand must turn downwards to keep the cue parallel.

I wouldn't get all this into my cablegram, unfortunately, but the essence of it all is there: the importance of the finish. You can only finish as I have described if your action is good. I would especially emphasise the turning down of the cue-hand at the wrist. If the wrist is kept rigid to the end of the stroke, then it follows that the hand and the cue must lift upwards. To keep the cue dead horizontal the wrist must flex so that the front knuckle and thumb are facing where the cue-ball was and not some point above it.

I think most players worry too much about getting the ball into the pocket, and not enough about the actual striking. It might well be that more concentration on the finish of the stroke would result in less anxiety about where the cue-ball is going and therefore eliminate the tendency to wave the cue round the corner. Why not try this?

7 Eye on Which Ball

As long as I can remember, there has been controversy in the billiards and snooker world over which ball the eye should be fixed on during the actual strike – the cue-ball or the object-ball. In billiards, it did not seem to matter very much though arguments about the subject can be found in books seventy years old. But when snooker became the main game almost everyone began to favour looking at the object-ball.

I do myself but I am not quite so one-sided in my view of it as I used to be. I still have my eyes on the object-ball as the cue comes through but nowadays I look at the cue-ball until the last split second. In fact, the cue has practically started to move in the strike when my eyes, for the last time, leave the cue-ball and go to the object-ball.

The reason is this: we are all making snooker more of an exact science every year and one of the things we now pay great attention to is precise striking of the cue-ball. We now know that if the cue-ball is struck as little as one sixteenth of an inch to left or right of centre in a medium or slow-medium pace shot when the ball has to travel over four feet, some side has been applied and the track of the ball will not be true. It will wander off. Spin has been used. In the case of the novice who cues so poorly that at times he miscues as the tip slides off the edge of the ball, the chances are that he never strikes dead centre, that every ball carries side, and that he only pots his ball when one error corrects another or the distance is too short for the side to take effect.

Central striking is essential for accuracy and as one is 'waggling' and adjusting the cue must be moving away from the central point of striking. Therefore, the eyes must be continually coming back to ensure an accurate contact. After all, if you put side on the cue-ball when you don't know it or intend it, what chance have you of potting your ball?

I am certain too that looking at the object-ball creates a temptation to try to steer it into the pocket by waving the cue away from it. This temptation cannot arise if one just refuses to look at the object-ball when striking. I have experimented in potting at times by getting my direction and my stance firmly settled, looking carefully at each ball in turn, and then striking with my eye on the cue-ball and I would not go into the witness box and say I potted any the worse.

Naturally, I am not recommending that snooker players at large should change over to the 'eye on the cue-ball' method but there are many players who could profit by it. For instance, there is the player who cannot play a forcing shot or a heavy screw shot without fluffing the pot. There are also many players who cannot screw a ball more than an inch and who think there must be something special about the cue or the tip, when they see a good player screw back three or four feet.

Their trouble is in inaccurate striking – they are not hitting the ball where they think they are. If you are one of these players, next time you have a simple pot and wish to screw back a couple of feet, get your stance and alignment adjusted, lower the butt of the cue as well as the tip, watch the tip strike the bottom of the ball and go right through it. You will find the object-ball has gone cleanly into the pocket and your screwing power will surprise you. I think, too, that applying maximum side, as is sometimes necessary, is never safe unless the eye is on the cue-ball at contact.

8 The Shots

SCREW

As so many strokes in snooker are played with screw, I should mention that all good players turn the bridge hand over for this type of stroke. I doubt if one amateur in a thousand does so, and perhaps this is why the amateur has such difficulty in deep screwbacks of some distance. Normally the bridge rests on the tips of the four fingers and on the two large pads at the base of the hand. Thus, with the thumb cocked, the channel for the cue is roughly an inch from the cloth which enables you to strike the ball centrally. If you wish to hit it higher up for topspin, you should raise the channel by drawing the fingers up closer, so that the stroke can still be made with a horizontal action.

But screw calls for hitting the bottom part of the ball. Here, the vast majority of players use the normal bridge and consequently strike a downward blow. This means two things: the first is loss of spinning action and the second is inaccuracy of direction, and is probably the chief cause of so many pots being missed when screw is applied.

The bridge for a shot with screw is simple enough. Make the normal bridge and then turn the hand over onto the thumb. The hand is now resting on the fingerpads and the full length of the side of the thumb. Now the channel for the cue is as low as you can get it with this type of bridge and you are able to strike the bottom of the ball with a cue which is as near horizontal as you can hope for.

**Photo 19.
Bouclée
Bridge**

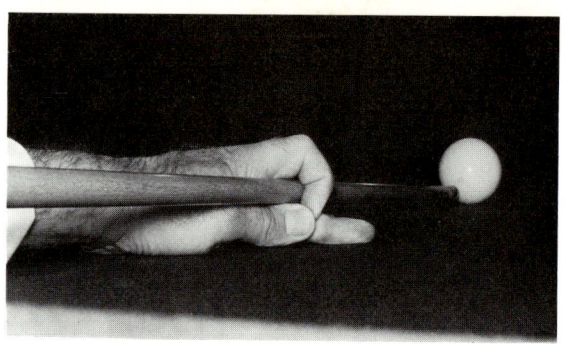

The bouclée bridge, usually referred to as the loop bridge, is principally used for powerful screw shots.
To apply screw (reverse spin) the cue-ball needs to be struck well below centre as shown. With the orthodox bridge there is sometimes a tendency for the tip to strike higher than one intends but the bouclée bridge, with the finger on top preventing the cue from lifting, is one means of ensuring that the intended low tip contact is in fact made.

Played this way, the cue can be thrust right through on a straight track without any fear of digging into the cloth and the spin will be far greater. At the same time, the accuracy of direction should not be affected.

With very little experiment you will find you can adjust the height of the bridge similarly for the stun shot in all its varieties and for a change you won't hope for backspin: you will know you are going to get it.

The loop bridge, a favourite in American pool and of some snooker players, should be used for deep screw only (Photo 19).

SIDE

A player must often use side but he should understand its difficulties. One is that to estimate its effect exactly is practically impossible and this means that it should be used only where there is plenty of room for error or where there is no room for error but no other way is possible.

Diagram 1.

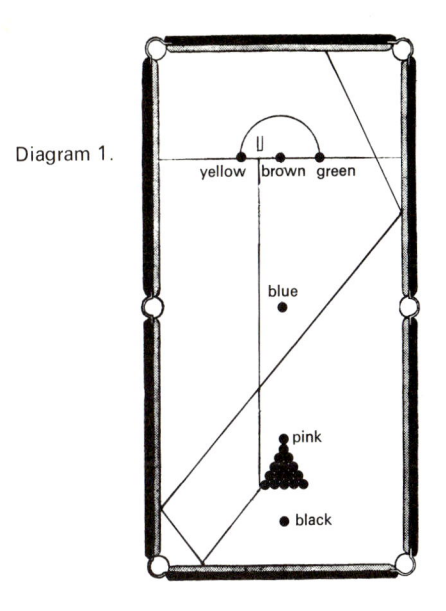

Taking the first point: it should always be used for the opening stroke, in which the top outside ball (usually the right) should be clipped with very strong running (right hand) side at half speed (Diagram 1). This brings the cue-ball round the top angle, across above the blue, safely behind the baulk colours. There are many other safety shots of a similar type in which the amount of side taken is immaterial. But in using side off a cushion to get out of a snooker, for example, the margin for error is very small indeed. This is a case for avoiding the use of side if possible.

When the object-ball to be potted is a long way off – say six feet or more – and it has more than a foot to go to the pocket, the use of side is again dangerous, for in six feet of travel the side may take the cue-ball off the line half an inch or more – unless it is going very fast – and thus result in the pot being missed.

What I have tried to explain is this: side is an invaluable ally, when used properly; but the moment you attempt accuracy with it at long distance you run into trouble.

To use side with maximum effectiveness, it is vital to

strike through the cue-ball and not across it. Do *not* address the centre of the cue-ball and *then* point your tip at the side. Imagine the cue-ball is an egg shell. For an ordinary stroke, the cue will go through the shell on one side, through the middle and out the other side in a straight line. The path of the cue when using side should be *parallel* to this line.

STUN

Stun is essentially a modified form of screw, or backspin. Whereas the idea of screw is to make the cue-ball recoil from the object-ball, the idea of stun is to have the cue-ball carrying just enough backspin to stop it dead on impact with the object-ball. This, of course, applies only to a straight shot. When the shot is at an angle, stun merely allows the cue-ball to leave the object-ball at a sharper angle than it would from a natural plain ball shot, but not as sharply as it would from a shot played with screw.

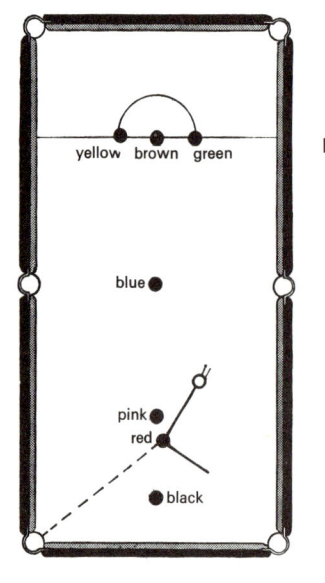

Diagram 2.

The point at which the tip should strike the cue-ball to apply stun varies according to the distance cue-ball and object-ball are apart. When these two balls are close, the tip contact may be halfway up the ball. When they are further apart, the tip strikes lower until at a distance of eight or nine feet, a full blooded screw shot, striking the cue-ball as low as possible, is necessary to stop the cue-ball dead. In diagram 2 for instance, the cue-ball would be struck just below centre to stun the red and hold position for the black.

SWERVE

Almost anyone who has been playing snooker for a year – not very long for this game – can swerve the ball a little. But the stroke is seldom used. So little is known about it among amateurs, apart from a rudimentary knowledge of how it is done, that it is not trusted and therefore not exploited.

To the expert, there is a whole range of fascinating strokes hidden in the swerve and even if you can't find time for experiment or practise, it will help you to know something about it.

The swerve is not just a method of putting side on a ball but a different type of blow altogether. The cue is raised at least 45 degrees – an important point because most players do not raise the butt high enough.

With the butt thus raised, the palm of the bridge hand must leave the table, so that the bridge rests solely on the pads of the four fingers. This means tense gripping with those pads on the cloth, for if the bridge wobbles the whole thing will flop. Having raised the butt and prepared for a well timed deliberate stroke, the cue-ball is struck to one side and *below centre*. This is another matter in which many players go wrong. They strike high. I find that the lower the ball is struck on the side, the greater the amount of swerve.

The tip of the cue should be used almost as if the cue was trying to chip or dig a piece off the ball. There is

Diagram 3.

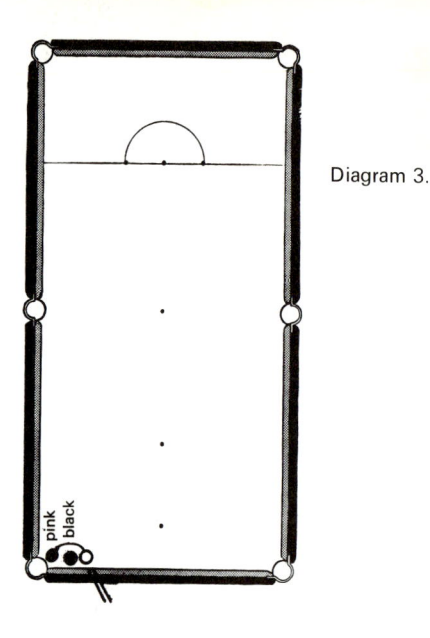

virtually no follow through but the tip must so grit itself into the skin of the ball that it is given the maximum amount of spin. The variety of effects from swerve arise from the effectiveness of the impact of tip on ball; on the speed at which the stroke is played; and the height of the cue butt. The higher the butt, and the lower the point of contact, the greater the degree of spin. If the cue is raised almost to the perpendicular it is possible to play a massé, a close-quarters shot in which the cue-ball may spin in an elongated semi-circle of no more than eighteen inches deep (Diagram 3).

Swerve, though, is basically a long distance affair, played necessarily at fair speed (not too great) for avoiding an intervening ball standing two and a half to four feet away, to hit an object ball six to ten feet away.

The arc taken by a swerved ball is deeper at the start. What happens is that the blow – assuming the ball is struck low on the right hand side – will drive it out sharply to the left and then the spin will operate so that

Diagram 4.

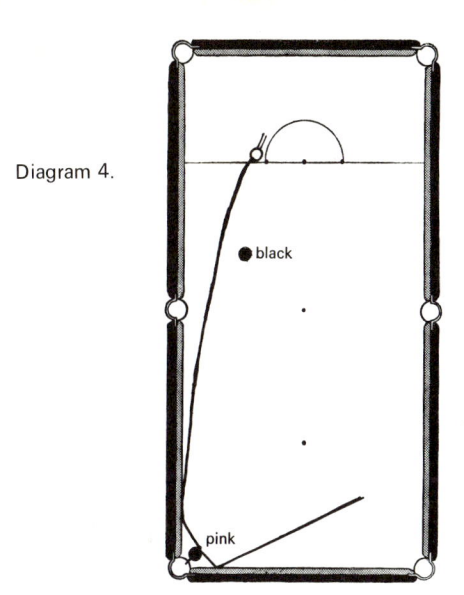

it turns back towards the right. But the second part of the journey is longer than the first – how much longer depends on the amount of spin.

It is possible to play a fairly slow swerve for quite a short distance, and indeed this can be a very pleasing stroke.

The swerve can be a life saver at times in snooker when, for example, one is so snookered that the centre pockets prevent the use of cushions to escape. It might happen, for instance, that one is snookered with the cue-ball in baulk, to a ball over a top pocket (Diagram 4). But I still consider the cushions to be almost always preferable to the swerve for playing out of a snooker, as the end result of the shot is much more predictable. The swerve, therefore, is to be regarded as the last resort, but a more than useful one.

Harry Burns (Widnes) a leading amateur. An excellent illustration of how to form a channel for the cue when it is necessary to make one's bridge on the cushion. Note how the tip of the second finger is used to keep the cue on line.

9 Touch and Feeling

Looking beneath the surface of the game of snooker, the person who understands it is struck at once by the immense gap between the ordinary player and the expert in the basic approach to the striking of a ball. To most club players the cue is a piece of wood and the ball is the object to be hit. True, by using side or screw the ball performs differently but that is as far as our club player goes. He merely endeavours to hit the cue-ball onto another and is pleased if he succeeds in potting several balls with successive strokes.

The expert regards the cue, the balls, the cushions and even the cloth as virtually living organisms. See a professional giving a demonstration of trick shots and you are amazed at the extraordinary way in which he can make a ball spin. He can use side to make an angle twice as wide as you can, and he can screw a ball the length of the table with ease – and without undue force – whereas you perhaps can screw no more than a dozen inches despite using your maximum power.

You suspect he uses cue-tips which you cannot buy. Well, certainly he regards the tip of his cue as vitally important, but he has no secret brand, no source not available to you. You will probably find he possesses a couple of dozen tips; these he has picked up, one here, one there. He does not use the same tip until it falls off or until it wears down to the ferrule; he changes it before a change is forced upon him. If the new one does not respond perfectly, he changes it at once.

A good tip has to have a softish surface with a hard base. Without being spongy it must hold onto the skin of the ball yet be solid enough to transmit the power. It must not weaken on one side (many do).

Any good player will have his own cue. See that it is properly balanced and keep it in a case when not in use. In fact, I do not regard anyone as a serious billiards or snooker player if he does not do this. But there are many who take good care of their cue but pay very little attention to the tip, although a cue is only as good as its tip – or as bad. It should be so responsive that the player is virtually feeling the ball itself when he strikes.

Old balls, stale cushions and worn cloths reduce the game to mere bashing. Club committees are often reluctant to buy new balls so long as the ones in use are not badly chipped. They also dislike facing up to paying for new cushions and cloths. The fact remains that until you have played under the sort of conditions we have in championships you do not know what snooker can be like. Balls in good condition have 'life'. Standard cushions and new cloths act vitally. A good cloth ensures true running, but it also presents delicate problems of 'nap' which the good player relishes.

All this explains why it is easier for me to score a century break on a match table than a fifty break on a club table which may have pockets like buckets. The professional, it has often been said, can make the balls do everything except talk.

There is a difference, too, in the feeling put into the stroke. The average player simply hits the ball, as accurately as he can and as near the required strength as he can. The professional plays the great majority of strokes during a break at short range and with screw and stun for position; and in playing these minutely accurate shots he manipulates the leather tip on the skin of the ball as delicately as a violinist. He does literally feel the spin being applied. Have you ever thought of it like that?

A professional's touch is epitomised in what is known as the 'soft screw'. In this shot the object ball is potted at an angle and screw is applied: but the stroke is less than medium strength so that the cue-ball's run is 'killed' within a couple of feet. To apply screw slowly is quite beyond the average player. The professional makes it look easy, and the secret of it is simply that he consciously spins the ball whereas the average player merely strikes it low.

In every stroke played, including the initial opening from hand, the professional seems to be using only half the power that the average player requires to get the same result. The reason is that he has learnt to use the resilience in the balls and the response of the cushions. And he does change his tip!

John Terry (Ystradgynlais), former British Junior Snooker champion. Note how the fingers are widely spread, and the lower arm is resting on the table bed for additional support.

10 Positional Play is the Key

It is true that I pot better than you do. I play more. I have studied the game and worked at it more. My action is now (or should be) so much in a groove that I can only miss if I assess the angle wrong. At any rate, that is the theory. It is not 100 per cent correct, because I am prone to the same unpredictable waywardness of the cue as you are, albeit to a lesser degree.

But if it came to a potting match pure and simple, so that we could each in turn place the white where we liked, I wouldn't be so very much better than you. Perhaps the most important reason why I pot more consistently than you do is that my pots are, on the whole, much easier than yours.

It all starts with the first red in the break. I go for that red with a diagram in my mind so that, if the shot comes off as planned, the cue-ball will be within a few inches of a certain spot, in good line for a colour. Provided I get my red and the stroke is well played, the colour will be quite easy. I planned it that way, because, when the colour is easy I can pot it with another diagram in my mind for the next red.

With all due respect, if you are an average player, you do not do that. The first red is by no means easy and for that reason you concentrate so much on potting it that if you succeed, there may be no colour to follow at all. This, you tell yourself (and your opponent) is very hard lines after so fine a red. In a way, yes. But it isn't the way to play snooker.

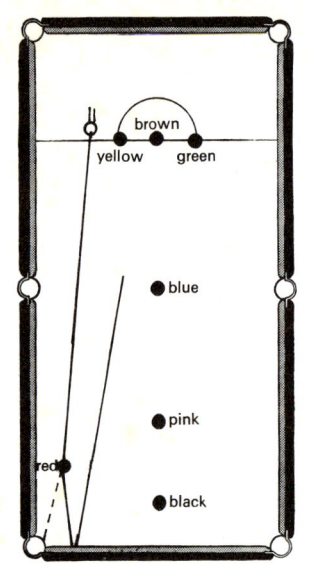

Diagram 5.

It's the way millions play, I know. Millions don't get any better, though they all want to. The golden gate to the big break, the break which shatters the opposition and wins matches, is through positional play – not merely potting with the idea of taking the black afterwards, but a thoroughly worked out scheme to leave the cue-ball so that the black will be easy.

For instance, there is that long, almost full ball shot from the baulk line, potting the red into the top pocket – a narrow, half closed pocket, a shot you nearly always over-cut (Diagram 5). A nasty shot for anyone. So you take extra care, concentrate very hard, play it gently and, if the red goes in, you find the cue-ball resting against the top cushion. Almost a hopeless scoring position. You score one point.

The professional may not even play it to get behind the black. In most cases he will strike firmly, with topspin, to bring the white back to the middle of the table for a choice of blue, pink or brown. That way, he probably leaves nothing if he misses and is sure of a colour if the red drops. He knows, too, that if the red is accurately struck it will drop whether it is hit soft or hard.

It does not matter which colour you ultimately choose to be on, but you must always shape your stroke with the object of being on some colour. Single points are not merely useless; they are disheartening. I have sat in clubs and seen players – and reasonably good players too – walk to the table and pot a red without even having considered what there might be to follow. On the other hand, what immense satisfaction there is to get a difficult red down and also find you have succeeded in getting into the position you had in mind.

The chief obstacle is mental: how to divide one's concentration between the job of potting the red and the control of the cue-ball. Very often the latter is quite complicated – you perhaps need a little screw, or stun, or side, allied to which must be the correct length. All this adds up to fine snooker. But let us consider the simpler shots, where no more is required than to pot your red with correct strength to get into position behind (and near to) the selected colour. This means, more often than not, using a cushion, perhaps two cushions.

Are you able to do this? Can you divide your mind when striking so that, although concentrating on the pot, you are also taking care to give the ball just enough, and not too much 'stick'? That, I suggest, is the most important thing to study for the vast majority of players who wish to improve.

The answer may be simpler than you think. When you reflect on it, you will agree with me that most average players strike too fast. They let the shot go before they are really ready. At the vital moment, they are not completely in control of the cue which is like a horse at the gate, anxious and pulling to get away. Most, if not all, first class snooker players let the cue go slowly, almost reluctantly, even when playing a power shot. That pause, or slowing down of the action just before striking, is the opportunity to gain control. It will also enable you to keep your head down and stop the cue waving off the line. But here we are dealing with the strength control, and this is the way you can obtain it. By that final pause, you will find you can control the run of the cue-ball surprisingly well. And you can take heart from the fact that you are better off missing five reds if the sixth goes in, and lands you bang on the black, than you are if you pot all six reds and have nothing to follow.

In short, you have made your colour an easy shot. That objective should always be prominent in your mind.

11 Checking up on Your Style

Although you cannot see yourself play (and what a pity this is) it is possible to check whether you are doing the essential things as you should. There are several ways of checking your action. For instance, you should lower your head so that your chin is within a quarter of an inch of your cue. If you do that, then the cue should ride against your necktie just below the knot. This is very important; so important that good players who play regularly find they wear out their ties by the constant brushing of the cue. Next time you get down to the shot, therefore, just make sure your cue is riding against your tie.

The next check of your action must be on general compactness, and here I suggest you ascertain where your cue hand finishes. A good horizontal cue action should result in your thumb banging into your ribs when the stroke is complete. I expect nine readers out of ten find that this does not happen.

Well, it should. It will if the cue, in addition to riding against the tie, rides also very close to the upper waistcoat pocket. If this is happening, then logically, as the cue is thrust through, the hand must follow the cue-tip and hence the thumb hits the ribs.

We are now taking the action to pieces, and in fact that is the best way to analyse your style for faults. You see, if the two pieces of advice I have just given you are not followed in your style, it must mean that you are playing with a hanging wrist – that is, away from your body and not down the line of the stroke. This must increase your difficulties enormously. It will also cause you to be erratic, because if you are playing with a hanging wrist, how do you know that it is always hanging the same distance away from the true line?

Now go farther back in the action. Your forearm should, at rest, hang vertically from the elbow, and when you move it, nothing except the forearm, hand and cue should move at all until the actual stroke. The pump handle action, moving the upper arm, is fairly common because the victims don't know they have this fault.

You should be able to check on this common fault simply by conscious feel. When making your preliminary waggles for free swinging, it is not difficult to know whether the upper arm is moving or not. Nothing should move except the forearm until the stroke is made, and then, of course, the upper arm must come down as the elbow follows through on the line.

The next check is on the finish of the cue, as distinct from the finish of the cue hand. Do you hold the cue absolutely on the line of the shot after it is made? If so, you are one in a thousand: but this is something towards which you must strive. Nearly all amateurs allow one of two things to happen: either the tip of the cue lifts into the lightshade or the cue tends to wave away from the line in the direction opposite to the pocket. The latter fault is very common when performing cut shots. The trouble with these bad finishes is that they are symptoms of a bad action and are apt to influence the action before the contact is made. Thus, unwanted side is inflicted and thus intended screw is never applied. The cue should finish on the line of the stroke with the tip either on the cloth or parallel and just above it. If you can achieve that, you may be fairly sure that the pot has gone down, unless it was an extremely difficult one.

Another check to be made from time to time is on your stance. You should know whether there is any movement in your feet, body or head as you strike and if there is, it must be put right without delay. The margin for error is little enough anyway and if you add the burden of trying to pot 'on the run', as it were, you will not have much chance. There are two sources of this trouble: one is bad body balance, caused by the weight being so distributed that toppling forward is all too easy in anxious moments. The actual point of balance, or invisible fulcrum, depends on your build – if you are short, you may well come forward over the knee, but if you are a six footer, like John Pulman then, like John, you will have to stand so that the weight is more over the straight (almost vertical) back leg. By the way, tall men often make the mistake of thinking they are more securely founded if they spread their legs wide, but this is not so. Pulman's feet are at least as close as mine are, and he must be five or six inches taller.

The other source of trouble, and a very common one, is failure to make a really secure bridge. Many players are satisfied to bunch up their fingers in a heap and poise the cue somewhere on top. You have to realise that the bridge hand is there to act as an anchor, together with the two feet, and that the pads of the fingers should be made to grip the cloth hard: this grip not only makes the channel for the cue immovable, but also helps to keep the whole body steady and, indirectly, to keep your head down.

I expect I have put more tasks for you in this section than you can remember, and I therefore suggest you sort out those most likely to tighten up your game. Never forget that the only real difference between you and me, in snooker, is that I stick to the fundamental principles rigidly. There aren't any mysteries or secrets.

Trevor Wells (Southampton), British Junior Billiards champion 1974. A left-hander with a nice easy style.

12 You Can Always Improve

I have proved several times that it is possible for a person of practically any age, so long as he plays snooker fairly regularly, to improve. And to improve quite a lot. When you look around the fifty or sixty men in your club whom you meet in the billiard room during the week, you can count on the fingers of one hand those who are improving – mostly players who are fairly new to the game. The rest play much as they did five, ten, fifteen years ago. Perhaps not quite so well.

Friends come to me at times for advice and I also play many a friendly game on my own table at home. Among my friends are men in their sixties, one is over 70. They all improve with a little coaching and if they take the trouble to have some quiet practice they improve a great deal. But not at once. When you settle down to regular practice along new lines, it is certain that your game will fall to begin with. You have got your game into a groove in which one fault corrects another. It takes time and patience to straighten it all out. There is no magic wand to real improvement. I can look you over while you play, tell you what you may be doing wrongly and show you how to do it correctly; but will it last?

Once a player said to me: 'The soft screw is the stroke I can never understand. It is so utterly beyond the understanding of the ordinary player; yet you professionals play it easily'. I told him that, once the stroke had been explained, it needed only practice and confidence. So I explained it, and he tried it, and after twenty minutes he potted his black at three quarter contact and made the

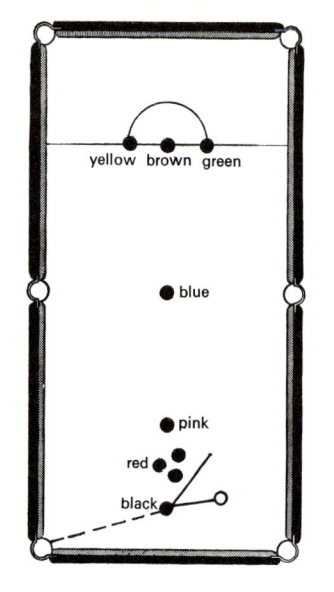

Diagram 6.

cue-ball curl back gently, all with the below medium shot (Diagram 6).

Instead of the cue-ball shooting away at right angles seven or eight feet, it described its little backward arc and stopped in two feet. But of course he has never been able to do it since, because this stroke, which is the supreme stroke in snooker, the acme of cue-ball control, really takes years to master.

A player can improve without practice, of course. Even a player of long standing, if he knows his fault and tries hard to correct it, can improve to that extent. But those who are really ambitious must be prepared to do some practice every day, perhaps for years.

All leading professionals have been through it. Walter Lindrum, the wonderful pre-war billiards wizard, used to tell how he stayed up until 2.00 am when his father and uncle, both champions, had gone to bed, in order to have the table in absolute quiet. He was eight years old then. At seventeen, he made his first four figure break.

Diagram 7.

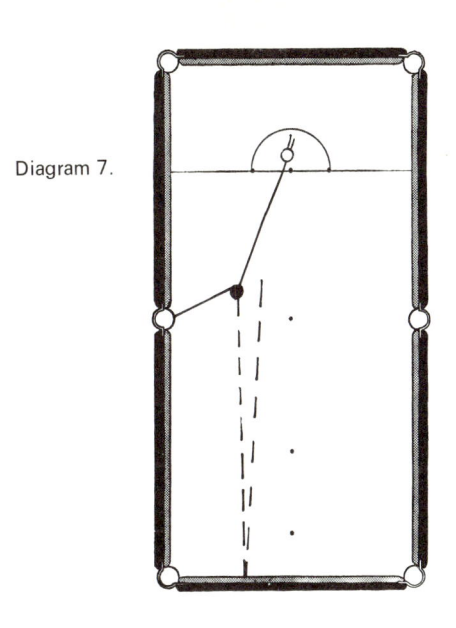

Still, it would be madness to ask you, my readers, to start that sort of life. You have other things to do. But if you can find the odd half hour, with a table to yourself, there are many forms of practice which break up the tedium. One is the losing hazard of billiards – playing in-offs into the centre pocket from hand to bring the object-ball down over the centre pocket again (Diagram 7). Wonderful for cue control.

For practice in follow through to cure the nervous stabbing action which creeps in at important moments in a game – set the cue-ball on the brown spot and place the brown halfway to a centre pocket, but below the straight; then practise potting brown, with plenty of follow through, rhythmically bringing the cue-ball back on the green (Diagram 8).

For dead straight potting, put the cue-ball on the baulk line, blue on its spot and pot it into the top pocket (Diagram 9). When you can do this reasonably well, introduce stun by degrees. A master player can sink the blue

Diagram 8.

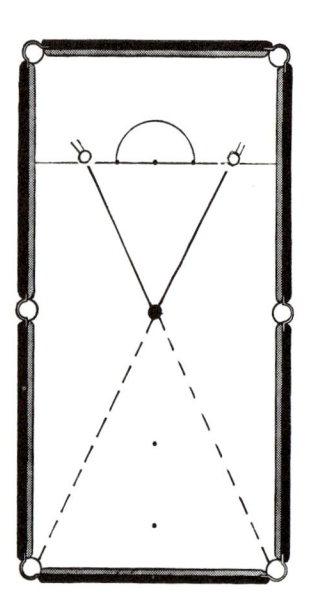

Diagram 9.

Diagram 10.

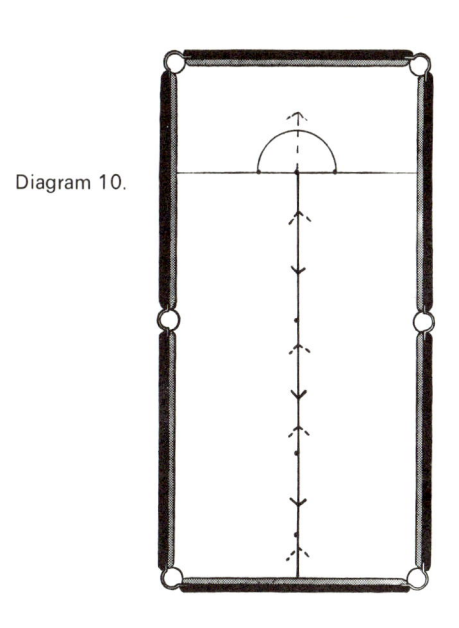

and stop the cue-ball dead on the blue spot. That, again, requires abundant practice. Do it from both sides as shown in the Diagram.

Most professionals like to start every practice by a few turns 'over the spots' – just playing a ball up and down the table twenty times or until assured that no side is being applied unknowingly and that striking is dead central (Diagram 10).

Practice is good for you for another reason. Most ordinary players allow some movement to creep in during a game – either a foot, or part of the body or the head is up too soon and this is a sign, as a rule, that the player is anxious and has played too quickly. In practice there is no anxiety; so that you begin to acquire the habit of rhythmic, controlled striking which is the inner key to everything. Practice, therefore, is especially valuable for the awkward shots – the ones you are apt to dash at because you dislike them, such as playing directly away from under a cushion and bridging over intervening balls.

Very definitely one can say you will never be better at these without practice.

Practice at screw shots can be infinitely varied and one could spend a couple of dozen sessions at nothing else without repeating precisely the stroke and its requirements. Deep screws, stuns, at many distances, forcing shots and soft screws – there is no end to them, and they constitute the major part of constructional snooker.

If you simply can't practise, however, there is one thing you can do to help your game along: take a solemn oath to yourself that you will never pot another red without combining it with a properly thought out positional play for a colour. You will miss more reds than usual, but you will get much more fun out of the game.

13 The Rules

General Rules

These General Rules, Technical Terms and Laws apply to Games played on an English Billiard Table. (Authorised by The Billiards and Snooker Control Council.)

THE TABLE

MEASUREMENTS

1. The B&SCC 12 ft. Standard Table: The slate bed of the table shall measure 12 ft. by 6 ft. $1\frac{1}{2}$ in. The edge of the cushions shall not project over the slate more than 2 in. or less than $1\frac{1}{2}$ in. The height of the table, from the floor to the top of the cushion rail, shall be from 2 ft. $9\frac{1}{2}$ in. to 2 ft. $10\frac{1}{2}$ in. There shall be pockets at the corners (the two at the Baulk end being known as the bottom pockets and the two at the spot end as the top pockets) and at the middle of the longer sides, and the pocket opening shall conform to the templates authorised by The Billiards and Snooker Control Council.

HEIGHT

POCKET OPENINGS

BAULK-LINE AND BAULK

A straight line drawn 29 inches from the face of the bottom cushion and parallel to it is called the Baulk-line, and the intervening space is termed the Baulk. The 'D' is a semi-circle described in baulk, with its centre at the middle of the baulk-line, and with a radius of $11\frac{1}{2}$ inches.

THE 'D'

SPOTS

Spots MARKED on the table are:

(a) THE SPOT, $12\frac{3}{4}$ inches from a point perpendicular below the face of the top cushion on the centre longitudinal line of the table;

(b) THE CENTRE SPOT, mid-way between the middle pockets;

(c) THE PYRAMID SPOT, mid-way between the CENTRE SPOT and the face of the top cushion; and

(d) THE MIDDLE OF THE BAULK-LINE – all four being on the centre longitudinal line of the table.

MEASUREMENTS

1. (a) The B&SCC 6 ft. Standard Table. – The slate bed of the table shall be not less than $\frac{1}{2}$ in. in thickness and shall measure 6 ft. by 3 ft. $1\frac{1}{2}$ in. The edge of the cushions shall project over the slate $1\frac{1}{2}$ in. There shall be pockets at the corners and at the middle of the long sides, and the pocket openings shall conform to the templates authorised by The Billiards

POCKET OPENINGS

and Snooker Control Council for 6 ft. standard tables.

BAULK-LINE AND BAULK — A straight line drawn $14\frac{1}{2}$ inches from the face of the bottom cushion and parallel to it is called the Baulk-line, and the intervening space is termed the Baulk.

THE 'D' — The 'D' is a semi-circle described in Baulk, with its centre at the middle of the Baulk-line and with a radius of $5\frac{3}{4}$ inches.

SPOTS — Spots MARKED on the table are:

(a) THE SPOT, 7 inches from a point perpendicular below the face of the top cushion on the centre longitudinal line of the table;

(b) THE CENTRE SPOT, mid-way between the middle pockets;

(c) THE PYRAMID SPOT, mid-way between the CENTRE SPOT and the face of the top cushion; and

(d) THE MIDDLE OF THE BAULK-LINE – all four being on the centre longitudinal line of the table.

BALLS

MEASUREMENTS — 2. The B&SCC 12 ft. Standard Table balls should be of equal size and weight, and of a diameter of $2\frac{1}{16}$ inches, within manufacturers' tolerance.

The B&SCC 6 ft. Standard Table balls should be of equal size and weight, and of a diameter of $1\frac{7}{8}$ inches, within manufacturers' tolerance.

THE CUE

2. (a) A Billard Cue as recognised by the B&SCC shall be not less than three feet in length and shall show no substantial departure from the traditional and generally accepted shape and form.

TECHNICAL TERMS

TO STRING — 3. (a) To string is to play together from the Baulk-line to the top cushion with the object of leaving player's ball as near as possible to the bottom cushion.

CUE BALL — (b) The cue ball is the ball of the striker; all other balls are object balls.

BALL IN HAND — (c) A player's ball is *in hand* when it is off the table.

TO PLAY FROM HAND — (d) To play from hand the striker must play the cue ball from some position on or within the lines of the 'D'.

BALL IN BAULK — (e) A ball is *in baulk* when it rests on the Baulk-line or between that line and the bottom cushion.

BALL OFF THE TABLE — (f) A ball is *forced off the table* which comes to rest otherwise than on the bed of the table or in a pocket.

STRIKER AND NON-STRIKER — (g) The person about to play or in play is termed the *Striker*; his opponent is the *Non-Striker*.

BALL IN PLAY — (h) The ball of the striker is *in play* when it has been finally placed on the table and struck with the tip of the cue (or spotted under the Rules of the game being played), and remains so until pocketed. The ball of the non-striker is *in play* when it has been spotted under the Rules of the game being played. Other balls are in play when spotted and remain so until pocketed. Any ball which is forced off the table becomes out of play.

A STROKE (i) A Stroke is made by a player touching his ball, or striking his ball when it is in play, with the tip of his cue. No stroke is completed until all the balls have come to rest and the player is ajudged to have left the table.

A BREAK (j) A Break is a series of consecutive scoring strokes made in any one turn.

A CANNON (k) A Cannon is made when the striker's ball makes contact with two other balls.

WINNING HAZARD (l) A Winning Hazard is made when a ball, other than the cue ball is pocketed after contact with another ball.

LOSING HAZARD (m) A Losing Hazard is made when the cue ball is pocketed after contact with another ball.

A MISS (n) A Miss is a stroke where the cue ball fails to touch any other ball; or in Billiards where the cue ball, when played from hand, strikes any part of a ball in baulk without first hitting a ball or cushion out of baulk; or where the cue ball is struck more than once before contact with another ball.

SPOT OCCUPIED (o) A spot or position is said to be *occupied* if a ball cannot be placed thereon without touching or disturbing another ball.

THE FALL (p) The curved edge of the bed of the table forming the mouth of the pocket is called the fall.

FIRST IMPACT OF CUE BALL 4. The first impact of the cue ball shall govern all strokes.

BALL PROPERLY SPOTTED 5. A ball is not considered to be spotted unless it has been placed by hand on its prescribed spot.

A FAIR STROKE 6. All strokes must be made with the tip of the cue. The ball must be struck, and not pushed. The ball must not be struck more than once in the same stroke either before or after contact with another ball. At the moment of striking, one of the player's feet must touch the floor. A ball or balls must not be forced off the table.

A FOUL STROKE 7. A foul stroke is one made in contravention of any Rule of the game being played (see Sectional Rules).

BALL ON EDGE OF POCKET 8. If the ball which falls is part of the stroke, that stroke shall be void, the balls placed in their original position and the stroke replayed. If the ball is not an integral part of the stroke, the stroke shall stand and the ball which fell only shall be replaced. If it balances momentarily on the edge and falls in, it must not be replaced.

BALL MOVED BY OTHER AGENCY THAN PLAYER

9. If a ball is disturbed otherwise than by the player, it shall, if moved, be placed on the table by the referee on the spot which, in his judgment, the ball had, or if moving, would have occupied. This rule covers the case in which a non-striker or non-player causes the striker to touch or move a ball. The player shall not be responsible for any disturbance of the balls by the referee or by the marker.

CONDUCT OF NON-STRIKER

10. The non-striker shall, when the striker is playing, avoid standing or moving in the line of sight; he should sit or stand at a fair distance from the table. He may, in case of his enforced absence from the room, appoint a substitute to watch his interests, and claim a foul if necessary.

PENALTIES

11. If during a stroke any rule is contravened the striker (a) cannot score, (b) loses his turn, (c) forfeits such points as are exacted under the Rules of the game being played.

BALLS CHANGED

12. The set of balls may be changed during a game, by consent of the players or by decision of the referee.

ORDER OF TURN

13. The players shall determine the order of play by stringing or by lot; the order of play shall remain unaltered throughout the game. The game does not

COMMENCEMENT OF GAME

commence until the cue ball has been finally placed on the table and struck with the tip of the cue, by the first player.

THE REFEREE

14. (a) The Referee shall be the sole judge of fair or unfair play, and shall be responsible for the proper conduct of the game under these Rules, and shall, of his own initiative, intervene if he sees any contravention. He shall, on appeal by a player, and on appeal only, decide any question of fact connected with play. (The referee on appeal if a ball is in or out of baulk shall only give a decision when the player is in hand.)

(EXAMPLES: If a ball touch the striker's ball; if it is properly placed to play from hand; or if properly spotted.)

If he has failed to observe any incident, he may take the evidence of the spectators best placed for observation, to assist his decision.

He shall decide all questions arising between the players on the interpretations of these rules.

The referee shall not give any advice or express opinion on points affecting play.

(EXAMPLES: The referee should not offer an opinion as to whether there is room for a ball to be spotted if pocketed by a stroke about to be played. If the striker plays from hand outside the limits of the 'D', the referee shall not warn him before the stroke is played, but shall award the foul immediately afterwards.)

THE MARKER

14. (b) The Marker shall keep the score on the marking board, and assist the referee to carry out his duties.

PLAYER'S CONDUCT

15. For refusing to continue the game when called upon by the referee to do so, or for conduct which, in the opinion of the referee, is wilfully or persistently unfair, a player shall lose the game, and is liable to be disqualified for any future competition held under the control of The Billiards Association and Control Council, or its Affiliated Associations.

THE SPECTATORS

16. Spectators should not interfere with the game, the players, the marker, or the referee.

THE PUSH STROKE

A Push Stroke is a foul and is made when (A) the tip of the cue remains in contact with the cue ball when the cue ball makes contact with the object ball, or when (B) the tip of the cue remains in contact with the cue ball after the cue ball has commenced its forward motion. Penalty in Billiards: None. In conjunction with a miss one away. In Snooker: Value of the ball 'on', or value of the ball struck, or value of the ball pocketed, whichever is the higher.

THE JUMP SHOT

The Jump Shot is a foul in which the cue ball is made to jump over any ball whether by accident or design. Penalty in Billiards: None. In conjunction with a miss, one away. In Snooker: Value of the ball 'on', or value of the ball struck, or value of the ball pocketed, whichever is the higher.

The Rules of Snooker

The General Rules, when not conflicting with any of the following Rules, govern this Game. (Authorised by The Billiards and Snooker Control Council.)

DEFINITION OF GAME

1. The game of SNOOKER (or Snooker Pool) is played on an English Billiard Table, and may be played by two or more persons, either as sides or

independently. It is a game of winning hazards; cannons are ignored. The winner is the player or side making the highest score, or to whom the game under Rule 14 is awarded.

THE BALLS

NUMBER IN SET

2. The set of balls should be twenty-two in number, consisting of fifteen reds, one black, one pink, one blue, one brown, one green, one yellow, and a white ball, which is called the cue ball. In the game on the B&SCC 6 ft. Standard Table the set of balls shall be seventeen in number, consisting of ten reds, one black, one pink, one blue, one brown, one green, one yellow, and a white ball, which is called the cue ball.

TECHNICAL TERMS

3. (a) The white ball is referred to as the *cue ball*; the yellow, green, brown, blue, pink and black, as the *pool balls*, or *colours*; the red (or pyramid) balls, as *reds*.

BALL FORCED OFF TABLE

(b) Any ball which is forced off the table becomes out of play, but, with the exception of a red ball, is immediately replaced upon its allotted spot.

BALL 'ON'. TO PLAY AT BALLS

(c) A player is said to be *on* a ball when such ball may be lawfully struck by the cue ball under these Rules. He is *on* a pool ball nominated under Rules 5 and 10.

PLAYER SNOOKERED

(d) A player is said to be *snookered* with regard to any ball when a direct stroke in a straight line of the cue ball to any point of such ball is obstructed by any ball which is not *on*. If a player is *in hand* after a foul, he cannot be *snookered* with regard to any ball that is *on*, if he can get a direct stroke in a straight line from some part of the 'D' (*i.e.,* a clear ball).

When the ball *on* is snookered by more than one ball, the effective snookering ball is the one nearest to the cue ball.

CUE BALL ANGLED

(e) The cue ball is said to be *angled* when the corner of the cushion prevents a stroke being made, in a straight line, directly on any part of all balls that may be lawfully struck.

NOMINATED BALL

(f) A *Nominated Ball* is the object ball which the striker declares he undertakes to strike with the first impact of the cue ball.

PLACING THE BALLS

4. Fifteen reds in the form of a triangle, the ball at the apex standing as near to the pink ball as possible, without touching it; the base being parallel with and nearest to the top cushion: BLACK on the BILLIARD SPOT; PINK on the PYRAMID SPOT; BLUE on the CENTRE SPOT; BROWN on the MIDDLE of the Baulk-

line; GREEN on the LEFT-HAND and YELLOW on the RIGHT-HAND corner of the 'D'.

MODE OF PLAY

5. Players must first determine by lot, or other convenient method, the order of their turn, which must remain unaltered throughout the game. The first player shall play from hand. The cue ball shall strike

FIRST STROKE

a red as the initial stroke of each turn, until all the reds are off the table. The value of each red, lawfully pocketed by the same stroke, is scored. For the next stroke of the turn (if a score is made) the cue ball shall strike a pool ball, the value of which (if lawfully pocketed) is scored. The game is continued by pocketing red, and pool balls, alternately, in the same turn. If the striker fails to score, the player next in turn plays from where the cue ball came to rest. If

CUE BALL POCKETED

the cue ball is pocketed or forced off the table, the next player plays from hand. Once the cue ball has come to rest on the table after a foul has been committed it must be played from where it has come to rest. Each *pool ball* pocketed or forced off the table,

RE-SPOTTING THE BALLS

must be re-spotted before the next stroke, until finally pocketed under these Rules. If the player who lawfully pockets the last red, pocket any pool ball with his next stroke, this ball is re-spotted. Other-

LAST RED POCKETING

wise (reds being off the table) the pool balls must be struck by the cue ball in the progressive order of their values, and *if lawfully pocketed* are not re-spotted.

POOL BALLS NOMINATING INTENTIONAL MISS

When requested by the referee a player must state which ball he is *on*. He is advised to do so for his own protection. An intentional miss shall not be made. The player shall, to the best of his ability, endeavour to strike a ball that is *on*.

FIRST IMPACT

The first impact of the cue ball shall govern all strokes.

EXAMPLE. A player *on* blue makes the first impact with the cue ball on the blue, the cue ball then strikes the black or any other ball and goes into a pocket, the player is penalised five points, the value of the blue, the ball on which the cue ball made the first impact.

BALL VALUES

6. The scoring values of the balls are: red = 1, yellow = 2, green = 3, brown = 4, blue = 5, pink = 6, black = 7.

RE-SPOTTING POOL BALLS

7. The striker must see that every ball required to be re-spotted is properly placed before he plays his stroke. *Reds* are never re-spotted. Any pool ball pocketed by a foul stroke is not deemed to have been lawfully pocketed, and shall be re-spotted. If the spot, named in Rule 4 for each pool ball, is occupied when such ball shall be placed thereon, the ball shall

be placed on the spot first named in Rule 4, that is then unoccupied, *i.e.,* if the spot allocated to the yellow is occupied by another ball, after the yellow has been pocketed, then the yellow ball is to be placed on the black spot, or, if that is occupied, then on the pink spot, and so on. If all the spots are occupied, any pool ball other than the black and pink shall be placed as near its own spot as possible between that spot and the *nearest part* of the top cushion without touching another ball. In the case of the black and pink balls being potted and all the spots are occupied, they shall be placed as near as possible to their own spots, up the table, on the centre line of the table, and without touching another ball. If the space between the black spot and the top cushion is occupied, the black ball shall be placed as near as possible to the black spot, on the centre line of the table, below its spot, and without touching another ball. Similarly if the space between the pink spot and the top cushion is occupied, the pink shall be placed as near as possible to the pink spot, on the centre line of the table, below its spot, and without touching another ball.

BALLS STRUCK SIMULTANEOUSLY OR POCKETED IN ONE STROKE

8. Two balls (other than two reds or the ball *on* and the ball nominated under Rule 10) must not be struck simultaneously nor pocketed by the same stroke.

NOTE: Any number of red balls may be pocketed by one stroke made in accordance with these rules.

CUE BALL TOUCHING

9. (a) If the cue ball is touching another ball which is *on*, the striker must play away from the touching ball without moving the latter, or he must be held to have pushed. The striker thus playing away from a ball *on* shall incur no penalty for a miss or for striking another ball, but he may lawfully pocket any other ball which is *on*. If he pockets a ball which is not *on*, he forfeits the penalty under Rule 12.

(b) If the cue ball is touching another ball which is not *on*, the striker must play away from such ball as in (a). If the ball *on* is missed, or another ball hit, the penalty as laid down in Rule 12 must be forefeited.

(c) In all cases where the cue ball is touching the ball *on* or touching a colour after a red has been potted, the referee shall state 'TOUCHING BALL' without being asked. If the cue ball is touching more than one ball *on* he shall, on request, state which ball(s) the cue ball is touching. He shall offer no other information.

EXAMPLES: (1) The *ball on is red*, cue ball is *touching red*, striker plays away from red without disturbing it, strikes and goes in off black. The penalty is four points, the value of the ball *on*.

(2) The *ball on is yellow*, cue ball is *touching yellow*, striker plays away from yellow without disturbing it, and pockets black. The penalty is seven points, the value of the ball *pocketed*.

(3) The *ball on is red*, cue ball is *touching black*, striker plays away from black without disturbing it, misses all balls and cue ball enters a pocket. The penalty is four points, the value of the ball *on*.

(4) In the case of the striker, playing away from black, missing all reds and striking blue he is penalised five points.

SNOOKERING AFTER A FOUL

NOMINATED BALL

NOMINATED BALL AND BALL 'ON' POCKETED

SNOOKERED BY THE NOMINATED BALL

MISSING THE BALL NOMINATED

10. After a foul stroke, if the striker be snookered, (a) *with regard to all reds*, he is then *on* any ball he may nominate, and for all purposes such nominated ball shall be regarded as a red, except that, if pocketed, it shall be spotted. (b) After a foul stroke, if the striker be snookered (*reds being off the table*), *with regard to the pool ball on*, he is then *on* any ball he may nominate, and for all purposes such nominated ball shall be regarded as the ball *on*, except that should it be lawfully pocketed it shall be spotted, and the player shall continue his break on the ball he was *on*, but for being snookered. If, as a result of playing on the nominated ball, the ball *on* be pocketed, it shall be scored and the player continues his break. Should both the nominated ball and the ball *on* be pocketed by the same stroke, only the ball *on* shall be scored, and the player continues his break. The nominated ball only shall be re-spotted.

Should the striker leave the opponent snookered by the nominated ball it is a foul stroke, except when only pink and black remain on the table.

Should the striker fail to hit the ball nominated under this Rule it is a foul stroke.

CUE BALL ANGLED

11. If the cue ball is angled it must be played from where it lies; but if angled after a foul, it may be played from hand, at the striker's discretion.

PENALTIES

12. A player who contravenes any Rule of this game (a) cannot score; (b) loses his turn; (c) forfeits such points as are exacted in these Rules – which are added to his opponent's score; (d) in addition, the striker has the option of playing from where the balls have come to rest, or requesting the opponent to play the stroke; (e) minimum penalty for any infringement is four points.

FOUL STROKES

13. The player contravenes these rules by the following acts (among others):

(a) By making a losing hazard. Penalty, value of ball *on*, or value of ball struck, whichever is the higher.

(b) By causing the cue ball to strike a ball he is not *on*. Penalty, value of the ball struck, or value of the ball *on*, whichever is the higher.

(c) By making a miss. Penalty, value of ball *on*.

(d) By snookering his opponent with the nominated ball after a foul stroke, except when only pink and black remain. Penalty, value of the ball *on*.

(e) By striking simultaneously or pocketing with one stroke two balls, except two reds, or the ball *on* and the ball nominated. Penalty, highest value of the two struck, or pocketed.

(f) By moving an object ball in contravention of Rule 9 (Cue ball Touching). Penalty, value of the ball *on*, or value of the ball moved, whichever is the higher.

(g) By forcing a ball off the table. Penalty, the value of the ball *on* or the value of the ball forced off the table, whichever is the higher.

(h) By pocketing any ball not *on*. Penalty, value of the ball pocketed, or value of the ball *on*, whichever is the higher.

(i) For playing with other than the cue ball. Penalty, seven points.

(j) By playing at two reds in successive strokes. Penalty, seven points.

(k) By using a dead ball to test whether a ball will pass another, or go on a spot, or for any other purpose. Penalty, seven points.

(l) By playing with both feet off the floor. Penalty – value of the ball *on*, or value of the ball struck, or value of the ball pocketed or value of the ball impropertly spotted, whichever is the higher.

(m) By playing before the balls have come to rest, or before they have been spotted or when wrongly spotted. Penalty, value of the ball *on*, or value of the ball struck, or value of the ball wrongly spotted, or value of the ball pocketed, whichever is the higher.

(n) By striking or touching a ball whilst in play, otherwise than with the tip of the cue. Penalty, value of the *ball struck* or *touched*, or value of the ball *on*, whichever is the higher.

(o) By playing improperly from hand. Penalty, value of the ball *on*, or value of the ball struck, or value of the ball pocketed, or value of the ball improperly spotted, whichever is the higher.

(p) Push Stroke. Penalty, value of the ball *on*, or value of the ball struck, or value of the ball pocketed, whichever is the higher.

(q) Jump Shot. Penalty, value of the ball *on*, or value of the ball struck, or value of the ball pocketed, whichever is the higher.

(r) By playing out of turn. Penalty, value of the ball *on*, or value of the ball struck, or value of the ball pocketed, whichever is the higher.

OFFICAL DECISIONS

Only the referee is allowed to clean a ball on the table. He should do so at a player's request.

It is the striker's responsibility to see that the balls are correctly spotted before playing his stroke.

If the referee considers that a player is taking an abnormal amount of time over his stroke, with the intention of upsetting his opponent, the referee should warn him that he runs the risk of being disqualified if he pursues these tactics.

A player should not be penalised if, when using the rest, the rest head falls off and touches a ball.

Unless a foul stroke is awarded by the referee, or claimed by the non-striker, before the next stroke is made, it is condoned.

If the striker plays with the balls improperly spotted, he scores all points made until the foul is awarded by the referee, or claimed by the non-striker.

The referee should not give any indication that a player is about to make a foul stroke.

If the striker makes a miss, the referee can order him to replay the stroke penalising him the requisite forfeit for each miss, but he scores all points in any subsequent stroke.

When awarded a free ball a player need only nominate the ball he intends to play, when requested to do so by the referee.

If at the opening stroke of a game the striker fails to hit a red, the next player plays from where the cue ball has come to rest.

A SNOOKER

A player must be able to strike both sides of the ball *on* free of obstruction from any ball or balls not *on*. It virtually means the diameter of a ball on either side of the ball *on*.

If a player is colour blind, the referee should tell him the colour of a ball if requested.

A referee must declare when a player has a free ball without appeal from a player.

EXAMPLES OF FOUL STROKES

EXAMPLES: (1) *Red is the ball on*, striker fouls *the black* with his cue or otherwise, the penalty is seven points, the value of the *ball fouled*.

(2) *Black is the ball on*, striker fouls *a red* with his cue or arm, the penalty is seven points, the value of the *ball on*.

(3) A player pots the *pink* and before it is properly spotted he pots a *red* ball – what is the penalty?

Decision: 6 points for playing with the balls not properly spotted (value of the ball not properly spotted).

WILFUL EVASION OF SPIRIT OF RULES

If a game is awarded to a player under Rule 15 GENERAL RULES, the offender shall lose the game, and forfeit all points he may have scored, or the value of the balls on the table (red = 8 each) whichever is higher.

END OF GAME AND TIE

14. When only the black ball is left, the first score or forfeit ends the game, unless the scores are then equal, in which case the black is spotted, and the players draw lots for choice of playing at the black from hand. The next score or forfeit ends the game. In games (whether individuals, pairs or teams) where aggregate points decide the winner, it is only when the scores are equal **as a result of the last frame**, that the black is re-spotted. The next score or forfeit ends the game.

FOUR-HANDED SNOOKER

Rules of Snooker apply.

In a four-handed match at snooker whether it be on frames or on aggregate points, each side shall open alternative frames, but the order of play shall be determined at the commencement of each frame. Players may change order of play at the beginning of each frame which must be maintained throughout that frame.

If a foul is committed and a request is made to play again, the player who committed the foul plays again, and the order of play is maintained.

When a game ends in a tie Snooker Rule 14 is applied. The pair who play the first stroke have the choice as to which player plays that stroke. The order of play must be maintained as in the frame.

14 Useful Information

ORGANISATIONS

The Billiards and Snooker Control Council
   Alexandra Chambers
   32 John William Street
   Huddersfield
   West Yorkshire

Publishes the full rules of billiards and snooker, copies of which may be obtained from them at £1 including postage and packing. They also act as the English amateur governing body and organise a coaching scheme for young players.

The International Billiards and Snooker Federation
Sec: L Oldham
   Alexandra Chambers
   32 John William Street
   Huddersfield
   West Yorkshire

The governing body for World Amateur Championships.

The World Professional Billiards and Snooker Association
Sec: S M Green
   77 Charlemont Road
   West Bromwich
   West Midlands

The governing body of the professional game.

Women's Billiards Association
Sec: Miss T Hindmarch
   72 Ravensbourne Park
   Catford
   London SE6 6X2

Organises annually Women's Amateur Championships.

Other national governing bodies include:

Scottish Billiards Association
Sec: John Waugh
   Rubismore House
   2 Cambridge Street
   Edinburgh

Welsh Billiards and Snooker Association
Sec: John Parker
   80 Shirley Drive
   Merthyr Tydfil
   Mid Glamorgan

BOOK LIST

Books

Winning Snooker by Eddie Charlton (Macmillan).
Complete Snooker by Joe Davis (W H Allen).
The Breaks Came My Way by Joe Davis (W H Allen).
Better Billiards and Snooker by Clive Everton (Kaye and Ward).
Billiards and Snooker by Jack Karnehm (Pelham).
Understanding Billiards and Snooker by Jack Karnehm (Pelham).
Snooker by Ted Lowe (EP Publishing).
Tackle Snooker by John Pulman (Stanley Paul).
Classic Snooker by Ray Reardon (David and Charles).

Spencer on Snooker by John Spencer (Cassell).
How To Become A Champion by Rex Williams (William Luscombe).

Magazine

Snooker Scene (editor: Clive Everton, Poulton House, 197 Hagley Road, Edgbaston, Birmingham B16 9RD). A monthly magazine which carries up-to-date reports on all major matches and tournaments, plus feature and instructional articles.

Tony Knowles (Bolton), former British Junior Snooker champion. Note the pronounced cocking of the thumb, and the way in which the base of the hand rests firmly on the table to make the bridge solid and immovable.

Glossary

(Terms refer to both billiards and snooker, or snooker only except where indicated.)

BREAK. A sequence of scoring shots.

BREAK OFF. The first shot of a frame in which the striker plays at the unbroken triangle of reds; in billiards, when the striker plays at the red to start the game.

CANNON (billiards only). A scoring stroke (value two points) in which the cue-ball contacts both object-balls.

CLEAR THE TABLE. A sequence of shots in which a player pots all the balls left on the table. (Also known as a clearance.)

CUE-BALL. The ball struck with the cue.

CUT. Potting by means of a thin contact.

DOUBLE. A shot by which an object-ball enters a pocket after contacting one or more cushions.

FREE BALL. If a player is snookered after a foul shot by his opponent he may nominate any colour as a red. If it is potted, he scores one and can then nominate a colour in the usual way. If all reds have left the table, the free ball is valued at the same number of points as the lowest valued ball on the table and the colours are then taken in sequence. For this purpose, a player is deemed to be snookered if he cannot hit both extremities of the object-ball.

FRAME. The name given to a game. Any number of frames, from 1 to 21, can make up a match.

FULL BALL SHOT. A contact in which the cue-tip, the centre of the cue-ball and the centre of the object-ball form a straight line.

HALF BALL SHOT. A contact in which half the cue-ball covers half the object-ball at the moment of impact.

HAZARD (archaic billiards term). A pot, in-off or combination of the two.

IN HAND. The situation in which a player may place his ball by hand in the D for his next shot.

IN-OFF. When the cue-ball enters a pocket after contacting an object-ball.

MAXIMUM BREAK. A break in which 15 reds, 15 blacks and all the colours are taken to total 147.

NATURAL ANGLE. The angle which the cue-ball takes after striking the object-ball without spin or more than medium strength.

POT. Propelling the cue-ball on to the object-ball to send the object-ball into a pocket.

PLANT. A position in which the first object-ball is played on to a second object-ball in such a way as to make the second object-ball enter a pocket.

SAFE POSITION. When the balls are so situated that a scoring stroke looks very unlikely.

SAFETY SHOT. A shot in which a player makes no attempt to score but intends to leave his opponent unable to score.

SCREW. Reverse spin. This is applied by striking the cue-ball well below centre.

SET. A position in which two object-balls are touching in such a way that the second ball will be potted with virtually any angle of contact on the first.

SHOT TO NOTHING. A position in which a player attempts a pot in such a way that he will be in position to continue his break if the pot is successful but will leave the cue-ball in a safe position for his opponent if unsuccessful.

SIDE. Sidespin. This is applied by striking the cue-ball to either right or left of centre.

SNOOKER. A position in which the cue-ball cannot hit an object-ball directly because of an intervening ball.

STUN. A shot in which the cue-ball is stopped dead (if the pot is straight) by striking the cue-ball just below centre. If the pot is not straight, the stun shot is used to widen the angle the cue-ball takes after striking the object-ball.

SWING. When the cue-ball follows a wide arc after contacting an object-ball at about half ball with considerable force; a shot usually employed to widen the angle to achieve a cannon or in-off.

Jonathan Barron (Mevagissey), former World Amateur Snooker champion. Note how he adopts a sideways action to play this shot with the rest. The lower right arm is horizontal to the table and the left hand keeps the rest securely anchored.